PAYCHECKS
AND
PROFITS

HOW TO MAXIMIZE EMPLOYEE BENEFITS, REDUCE YOUR TAXES, AND BUILD GENERATIONAL WEALTH

PAYCHECKS
AND
PROFITS

HOW TO MAXIMIZE EMPLOYEE BENEFITS, REDUCE YOUR TAXES, AND BUILD GENERATIONAL WEALTH

T.R. Smith

Published By
Top Line Press

Top Line
Press

Disclaimer

The information and advice in this book are not intended to replace the services of financial professionals with knowledge of your financial situation. The advice and strategies contained in this book may or may not be suitable for your situation. You should consult with a professional where appropriate. Neither the publisher nor the author shall be liable for any loss of any profit or any other commercial damages. All investments are subject to risk, and this should be considered before making any financial decisions.

This book is designed to provide information that the author believes to be accurate on the subjects it covers, but it is sold with the understanding that neither the author nor the publisher is offering individual advice for any specific portfolio or to any individual's particular needs or providing investment advice or other professional services such as tax, legal, or accounting advice. A professional's services should be sought if one needs expert assistance in areas that include investment, tax, legal, and accounting advice. This publication references performance data collected from past periods. Past results do not guarantee future performance.

Performance data and laws and regulations change over time, which could change the status of the information in this book. The data may not reflect the deduction of management fees or other expenses. This book provides historical data to illustrate the underlying principles. This book is not intended to serve as the basis for any financial decision, as a recommendation of a specific investment advisor, or as an offer to sell or purchase any security. Before investing, only a prospectus, read and considered carefully, may be used to offer, sell, or purchase securities. No warranty is made concerning the accuracy or completeness of the information contained in this book, and the author and publisher specifically disclaim any responsibility for any liability, loss, or risk, which is incurred as a consequence of the use and application of any of the contents of this book. The examples used in this book are for illustrative purposes only. The programs and benefits discussed in this book only apply in the United States of America.

In the chapters that follow, some names and identifying details have been changed.

This paperback edition first published in June, 2022

Paperback ISBN: 979-8-9858639-2-5
eBook ISBN: 979-8-9858639-3-2

All information provided is for general informational and educational purposes only and does not constitute investment advice. The information contained is intended by be truthful and not misleading, as required by FTC regulations. T.R. Smith is not a registered or licensed investment advisor with the SEC. T.R. Smith is not a certified public accountant. Only your registered/licensed financial advisor can give you personalized investment advice. T.R. Smith is not licensed/registered to make, and does not offer, personalized investment or financial advice as defined by the SEC. Investing involves substantial risks. Results are not guaranteed.

Published by Top Line Press

www.trsmithinvests.com

Dedication

For Anh and Jason and Laura

Table of Contents

Introduction 1

Part 1   Home Run Investments 15

    Chapter 1   401(k) with an Employer Match: 50% to 100% profit* 17

    Chapter 2   401(k) and IRA Tax Savings: 15% to 37% tax savings...........27

    Chapter 3   Employee Stock Purchase Plans: 15% to 70% profit............37

    Chapter 4   Health Care FSA: 30% profit or higher..43

    Chapter 5   Dependent Care FSA: 30% profit or higher............................47

    Chapter 6   Health Savings Accounts: 30% profit or higher.....................49

    Chapter 7   Commuter Benefits: 30% profit or higher...............................55

    Chapter 8   Credit Cards: 5% to 20% profit..61

    Chapter 9   Eliminating State Income Tax: 3% to 13% profit...................65

    Chapter 10 Put It All Together & Make Millions...71

Part 2   Build Generational Wealth..79

    Chapter 11 Real Estate: Own Your Home 81

    Chapter 12 Pensions..93

    Chapter 13 Custodial Accounts...99

    Chapter 14 529 College Savings Plans..103

    Chapter 15 Student Debt...109

    Chapter 16 Index Funds 113

Conclusion 117

About the Author..121

*Profit percentages and tax savings percentages are estimates and will vary based on individual circumstances.

INTRODUCTION

When I finished college and landed my first job, the world seemed like a welcoming place with endless possibilities. I was ready to live the good life. After two weeks on the job, I got my first paycheck and felt like I was punched in the gut. *Why is my take-home pay so low? How am I supposed to live off this?* I had just moved to San Francisco and my salary sounded reasonable when I was a starving student. But now, I was paying rent in an expensive city and watching my paycheck shrink thanks to taxes and other expenses I hadn't encountered before. Getting by was going to be difficult. Building a rich future was going to be even harder. As this new reality set in, I decided to focus my energy on saving more, paying less in taxes, and cracking the code to optimize my take-home pay. My journey took more than a decade and those hard-earned lessons have culminated in this book.

I like to tinker with things. I enjoy tinkering with everything from iPhone settings and smart thermostats to softer seat cushions in my car. It also includes my paycheck, investments, and tax returns. I like to find strategies and life hacks that make it easier to achieve important goals. I have always been fascinated with money and have tried to understand how some people accumulate so much of it. Over the years, I have tinkered with money and with different approaches to investing and I have learned some important lessons that I want to share.

Major stock market downturns that hurt a lot of investors made me wonder if there was another way to approach investing that allowed us to make big profits without taking big risks. I studied the stock market, the tax code, and employee benefits to identify certain types of investments and investment accounts that can give you a significant boost in building wealth.

Too many friends and coworkers have turned down free money from their employers and paid more than they needed to in taxes. I made some of those mistakes too; I learned some expensive lessons. After countless hours talking to experts, I decided to help people avoid common mistakes and, hopefully, create more wealth for themselves and their families.

My goal in writing this book is to help you achieve your financial goals by getting the best possible return on your investment. If you are new to investing, you will find useful material to help jump-start your journey to save and invest more. If you are already an experienced investor, you will find tips and tactics to improve your overall performance. If you find just one idea to implement, this book will have paid for itself many times over. If you begin saving and investing using the strategies I've laid out in the following pages, you can accumulate a great deal of wealth and achieve financial independence.

I received a Master of Business Administration (MBA) from one of the country's top universities and learned a great deal about money and investing. I have tried to condense key lessons I learned in the MBA program and the practical lessons I learned after business school into this book, to put more money in your pocket and reduce the risks that you take with your money.

One of the keys to successful investing in the stock market (or bond or real estate market) is to manage your emotions during the ups and downs. This is a lot easier if you can minimize the risk that you are taking with your money. It is even better when you can maximize the profits and tax savings when you make your initial investments.

Get Paid in Full

Are you ready for some surprising news? **You are not collecting your full paycheck**. Most likely, you are getting short-changed. Maybe the government is to blame for making things too complicated. Maybe your employer is to blame for not explaining your benefits in a way that everyone can understand. Maybe it is your fault for not spending a few hours or a few days to educate yourself on investing, taxes, and employee benefits. The good news is that this book is about to change that for you. It will unlock the hidden benefits in your contract with your employer, and ensure you start to get paid in full.

Doubling Your Dollars

Day 1	$1
Day 2	$2
Day 3	$4
Day 4	$8
Day 5	$16
Day 6	$32
Day 7	$64
Day 8	$128
Day 9	$256
Day 10	$512
Day 11	$1,024
Day 12	$2,048
Day 13	$4,096
Day 14	$8,192
Day 15	$16,384
Day 16	$32,768
Day 17	$65,536
Day 18	$131,072
Day 19	$262,144
Day 20	$524,288
Day 21	$1,048,576
Day 22	$2,097,152
Day 23	$4,194,304
Day 24	$8,388,608
Day 25	$16,777,216
Day 26	$33,554,432
Day 27	$67,108,864
Day 28	$134,217,728
Day 29	$268,435,456
Day 30	$536,870,912

There is an old legend about the origin of chess. When the inventor of the chess game showed it to the emperor of India, the emperor was so grateful that he asked the inventor to name his own reward. The main replied, "I would like one grain of rice for the first square of the chessboard, two grains for the next square, four for the next, eight for the next, and so on, for all 64 squares, with each square having double the number of grains as the square before."

The emperor agreed, thinking it was a small reward. After a week, his treasurer came to him and told him it would add up to an astronomical amount. It would be more rice than they could produce over many centuries.

Similarly, what would happen if you started with one dollar and found a way to double your money every day? That means you are getting a 100% return on your money every 24 hours. On day one, you have one dollar. On day two, you have two dollars. On day three, you have four dollars. It is not very exciting at first, but let's see what happens if we continue this for one month.

On day 21, you are a millionaire, and at the end of 30 days, you have over $500 million!

The point of this lesson is to understand that it doesn't matter how much money you start with. What matters is that you find ways to get a good return on the money you do invest.

While I don't know any methods that will allow you to double your money every day, I can show you how to use this mindset to become a millionaire if you understand where to look for the right investments. Becoming a millionaire is *not* a matter of luck or genius; it is just a matter of math.

Risk and Reward

Typically, low-risk investments offer a low reward. The money in your savings account may be secure, but you don't get much of a reward for keeping your money there. The bank might pay you 1%, or even less, each year in interest. You can put your money in the stock market, and you might get 8% or more most years. But there will also be years that you lose money. You could lose 50% or more in a bad year. There might be a 10-year period where your stock market investments lose money or just stay flat. While markets usually come back strong after a losing period, there are no guarantees as to when.

You could also invest in individual stocks. If you are lucky or have a talent for this, you might pick a stock that goes up 100% or even 300% or more in a single year. However, individual stocks can easily lose 50% of their value if they are especially volatile. A stock can even lose 100% of its value in a worst-case scenario. The opportunity for a big reward almost always requires you to accept a bigger risk. This is *risk versus reward* in the investing world.

But what if you could find investments that easily give you a return of 15% or 20% or even 100% on your money with little to no risk? These opportunities are hiding in plain sight; this book will show you how to exploit them.

Interest Rates and Compound Interest

As I write this book in the early 2020s, we are in a low-interest-rate environment. That means it is relatively easy to borrow money for a car or a house, but you might only earn a meager 1% on your money in a traditional savings account. Let's use 0% to 1% as the benchmark for a typical "risk-free" investment that does not fluctuate in value.

A US Government bond might only pay 1 to 3%. The real number can change every day, but keep this number in mind as another example of a low-risk investment.

The stock market typically returns anywhere from 8% to 12% in a year. There is no guarantee that the market will continue to perform this well, but we will use 8% as an example of what you might get when you invest in the stock market over the long term. This will also help us to evaluate how excited we should be for an investment that gives you 15% or more with little to no risk. To be clear, you should be VERY excited about this. Look back at the table of contents and you will see a preview of the many strategies to achieve this kind of profit.

The biggest problem with the stock market is that its value can fluctuate wildly from day to day and month to month. You will lose money some years, but you can usually make it back if you stay invested and ride out the storms. In reality, many investors only make about 3% to 5% per year by investing in stocks because they pay too much in fees and buy stocks when the market is up (or overvalued) and then sell stocks when the market is down (or undervalued). If you buy high and sell low, it is virtually impossible to make money in the market. The trick is to invest some money every month and not worry about what is driving short-term movements in the stock market. Stick with me through the book—we will discuss index funds and other simple strategies to invest wisely and ride out the market's ups and downs.

Think in Terms of *Percentages*, Not Dollars

You've probably heard about the bankers on Wall Street making millions (even billions!) of dollars per year managing money and making smart bets on which investments will go up and down. I won't try to dissect everything that's happening on Wall Street, but I want you to understand the fundamental reason why these "money managers" make so much money. A big part of the world of Wall Street is dedicated to the idea that you can "beat the market." In a typical year, the S&P 500 (a proxy for Wall Street's performance) may give you a return on your money of about 8%, but if you make some smart investments and get a return of 10%, you can earn a lot of money. I just want you to understand that a huge part of the financial world is built around trying to get a better return on your investments. Even a 1% or 2% improvement in your performance can be a BIG deal.

I mention the Wall Street money managers to get you thinking about how to score easy wins. If you can do something with your money that gets you a quick profit without any additional risk, you should seize the opportunity. That is what professional money managers do and why they can pay themselves millions of dollars. I want you to start thinking like a professional investor that gets excited about a high rate of return that allows you to outperform ordinary savings and investment plans.

Let's walk through one more illustration of compound interest. If you invest $1,000 and earn 10% that year, you will earn $100. Your new balance in the investment is $1,100. Let's say you earn 10% again the following year. Do you earn another $100? No. You earn more in the second year. You will earn $110 because you are earning interest on the interest you earned last year. The new balance will be $1,210. If you can fully understand and appreciate this fact, it will make you rich. If you continue to make contributions to your investments and interest compounds every year, there is no limit to how much money you can accumulate.

Let's take a look at some specific examples to get excited about the potential wealth creation from compound interest. The tables below show how much you can accumulate depending on how much you save and how much you earn on your investments.

Assuming 5% interest

Savings per year	5 years	10 years	15 years	20 years	30 years	40 years	50 years
$ 2,500	$14,505	$33,017	$56,644	$86,798	$174,402	$317,099	$549,538
$ 5,000	$29,010	$66,034	$113,287	$173,596	$348,804	$634,199	$1,099,077
$ 7,500	$43,514	$99,051	$169,931	$260,394	$523,206	$951,298	$1,648,615
$ 10,000	$58,019	$132,068	$226,575	$347,193	$697,608	$1,268,398	$2,198,154
$ 20,000	$116,038	$264,136	$453,150	$694,385	$1,395,216	$2,536,795	$4,396,308
$ 30,000	$174,057	$396,204	$679,725	$1,041,578	$2,092,824	$3,805,193	$6,594,462

Assuming 10% interest

Savings per year	5 years	10 years	15 years	20 years	30 years	40 years	50 years
$ 2,500	$16,789	$43,828	$87,374	$157,506	$452,359	$1,217,130	$3,200,748
$ 5,000	$33,578	$87,656	$174,749	$315,012	$904,717	$2,434,259	$6,401,497
$ 7,500	$50,367	$131,484	$262,123	$472,519	$1,357,076	$3,651,389	$9,602,245
$ 10,000	$67,156	$175,312	$349,497	$630,025	$1,809,434	$4,868,518	$12,802,994
$ 20,000	$134,312	$350,623	$698,995	$1,260,050	$3,618,868	$9,737,036	$25,605,988
$ 30,000	$201,468	$525,935	$1,048,492	$1,890,075	$5,428,303	$14,605,554	$38,408,981

Assuming 15% interest

Savings per year	5 years	10 years	15 years	20 years	30 years	40 years	50 years
$ 2,500	$19,384	$58,373	$136,794	$294,525	$1,249,892	$5,114,885	$20,750,934
$ 5,000	$38,769	$116,746	$273,587	$589,051	$2,499,785	$10,229,769	$41,501,869
$ 7,500	$58,153	$175,120	$410,381	$883,576	$3,749,677	$15,344,654	$62,252,803
$ 10,000	$77,537	$233,493	$547,175	$1,178,101	$4,999,569	$20,459,539	$83,003,737
$ 20,000	$155,075	$466,986	$1,094,349	$2,356,202	$9,999,138	$40,919,077	$166,007,474
$ 30,000	$232,612	$700,478	$1,641,524	$3,534,304	$14,998,708	$61,378,616	$249,011,212

As you can see, if you start early and invest wisely, there are many ways to accumulate millions of dollars. You can also see the importance of finding investments that give you a higher rate of return.

Home Run Investments

Everyone who invests is looking for a "home run." People secretly hope that a friend will give them a hot stock tip and the company they invest in will turn out to be the next Amazon or Netflix or Microsoft. Normally, when a friend or stockbroker tells you they have a potential "home run" investment, they are saying that they believe there will be a quick, short-term movement in a stock price. It might jump 10% next week based on strong earnings or it might jump 50% based on a report that a larger company wants to acquire it. It can be exciting to act on this and feel like you are part of a special club making easy money.

The problem is that these hot tips are impossible to consistently duplicate. Unless you are trading on inside information (which is illegal), you are mostly just guessing where the stock will go next. Virtually everyone already has the same information that you have. You may have good instincts about what could happen in the future, but others have already made some intelligent assumptions about where the stock will go next, and that is priced into the stock. If a lot of people think that earnings will be good, the stock has already been bid up in value. If the earnings are weaker than expected, you can take a big loss on this hot tip that you thought would be a home run.

The good news is that I am about to give you real-world examples of how you can invest in "**home run**" investments month after month and year after year. People typically define a "home run" investment as something that gives you a large gain in a short period of time. I define a home run investment as a strategy that is likely to give you an excellent rate of return with a relatively low risk. Some of these strategies will allow you to beat the market with little to no risk. When I use the term "home run" investments, I am generally referring to two different methods of making money. The first method gives you a short-term profit based on the money you contribute to an investment account. The second method gives you a reduction in taxes that puts money back in your pocket. In both cases, you are building wealth very quickly and doing so with less risk than most other types of investments. A 30% profit is a 30% profit, whether it comes from an increase in asset values or a tax savings. **A dollar saved is a dollar earned.** With home run investments, we will target 5 to 15% profits on the low end of the range, and 30 to 100% profits on the high end.

Just to be clear, I am not making any promises about buying an asset and holding it with a guarantee that it will increase in value in the future. Holding any investment carries some risk. However, you can use the tactics in this book to give yourself some significant profits. It will be up to you to decide whether you want to keep your profits in cash or invest in other assets after you exploit the short-term benefit. Keep reading and this distinction will be clear.

Generational Wealth

"Generational wealth" refers to assets that are passed from one generation of a family to another. This wealth can be transferred through an inheritance, a gift, or the payment of educational expenses. Imagine how different your life might have been if your parents bought you a high-quality car when you turned 16 and you were able to drive it for the next ten years without worrying about a car loan. Imagine how much money you could have saved and invested if your college tuition was paid for and you didn't have any student loans. What if your parents could have helped you buy a home after you started your first full-time job? Do you want to be able to do these things for your children in the future? Of course! This is why you want to build generational wealth. The opportunity to build great wealth for yourself and your family is probably a motivating factor for you if you are reading this book.

In **Part 1** of this book, I show you home run investments that allow you to make big profits and outperform typical investments. I also give you strategies to significantly reduce your taxes so that you can jump-start your savings and invest the extra cash. It only takes a little bit of planning. It includes:

- 401(k) employer match
- 401(k) and IRA tax savings
- Employee stock purchase plan
- Health care FSA
- Dependent care FSA
- Health savings accounts
- Commuter benefits
- Credit cards
- Eliminating your state income tax

In **Part 2**, I share additional strategies for other types of investment vehicles that allow you to build wealth over a longer period, creating generational wealth. This covers all the big topics that I wish I had known about when I finished college and started planning for the future. This includes:

- Real estate
- Pensions

- Custodial accounts
- 529 college savings plans
- Student debt
- Index funds

Problems You May Be Facing

Most people have some problems or concerns that stop them from investing and building great wealth. Let's review some of them before we get into the solutions in the future chapters.

Problem #1: Not knowing where to start. The result is they get started too late—or in some cases, never get started at all. You cannot let fear or lack of knowledge prevent you from achieving your goals. It can seem intimidating and like there's a lot to learn, but this book gives concrete examples of where you can put your money.

Problem #2: Thinking "It takes money to make money." This is simply not true if you follow the investing advice in this book. It is OK if you start with nothing. All you need is a job with some income.

Problem #3: Thinking you need to be especially smart to make a lot of investment income. You do not need to be especially clever. You only need to understand a few basic concepts and strategies to get a solid return on your money, and this book will show you how to do just that.

Problem #4: Thinking investing is just too risky. We all accept some risk in our lives. You take a certain amount of risk whenever you leave your house. You take a risk when you buy a house or invest your money. For people that have lived through the stock market crashes in 2001, 2008, and 2020, the risk (and reality) of losing a lot of money can sometimes seem unbearable. I lived through these market crashes and understand that many investors have significant scars from these major upheavals. I wrote this book because, even though I made plenty of mistakes along the way, I figured out a way to invest consistently and reduce risk by using the strategies I share in these pages.

The good news is that the market has recovered from all those short-term crises, and it is likely to recover from any future ones. The bad news is that many people have been scared out of the market because of the losses they took. They perceive investing as too risky. While there's no way to eliminate all risk, I can help you to *minimize* the risk and set you on the path to great wealth. More importantly, I will show you ways to get an **immediate return on your money** without taking big risks. This will accelerate your savings and give you an edge in your search for big profits.

Understand Your Employee Benefits

I have worked for several large companies. They were big enough that they had good benefits, a publicly traded stock, an entire department of human resource employees, and at least a few people dedicated specifically to company benefits. However, in each instance, they barely lifted a finger to explain what the company's benefits were and why employees should be excited to take advantage of them. Sometimes I got a brief presentation with a chance to ask questions. Sometimes I just got a big folder of papers and was told to read about the benefits and sign up whenever I was ready. This is a huge, missed opportunity for most companies, and because of that, most employees don't understand the potential wealth-building opportunities hidden in these benefits programs.

Employers should be jumping up and down in excitement to educate employees about why their company benefits can be the cornerstone of their employees' future financial planning. By the time most people finish school and take their first job, they haven't thought about taxes or compound interest or the risks associated with different investments. They're mostly just focused on getting a paycheck and paying the rent. As a result, employees are not signing up for basic benefits that would help them.

This book fills this void. I cover many different programs that help you to build wealth, reduce your taxes, and get a better return on your investment than any Wall Street professional can offer you. Be excited about your employee benefits and the opportunities to make some significant money from them.

I lost out on one benefit for a full year because I wasn't even aware it existed—a mistake that cost me about $2,000. Someone probably explained this benefit to me on my first day in the office, but no one ever reminded me or explained why it was important and how much money I could save. In that case, the benefit was only available after you had a child and I just wasn't focused on it; after all, we'd just had a baby.

You will get the most out of this book if you have a job with some benefits. But even if you don't, you'll still find a great deal of practical advice that applies to you and your future. You may decide that you want a job with certain types of benefits after you read this.

My Superhero Origin Story

I always liked money as a child—and I know I'm not alone in this. I loved getting visits from the tooth fairy and finding free money. I was always excited when I got a few dollars on my birthday or Christmas because it meant I could spend it on anything I wanted. I understood it opened possibilities. And I knew I could save up for something big!

My grandmother also taught me how to look for silver coins. The US government stopped making silver quarters and dimes and started using less precious metals. But if you knew how to look for the silver ones, it turned every interaction with loose change into a treasure hunt. Look at the edge of your quarter or dime; if it appears to be all white and silver, it may be an old silver coin and is worth much more than its face value. The same is true for half dollars. If you find a dime, quarter, or a half dollar from 1964 or earlier, hold onto it or take it to a coin dealer if you want to sell it. These silver coin hunts were some of my first interactions with free money and making a profit by keeping my eyes open and learning a few tricks.

Shortly after I was born, my grandfather put $100 into a savings account for me. When I was younger, I didn't understand what $100 could buy, but I thought it was exciting that I had any money in a bank somewhere. When I was in first grade, I got a birthday gift of $20, and my parents showed me that I could put that money into my savings account. We had a little passbook that showed how much money was in the account and how much the bank paid in interest. This was back when banks paid about 8% on savings or CDs (certificates of deposit). So, I made $8 in the first year just by letting the money sit there. Then I realized that I made even more than $8 in the following years because I earned interest on the interest that the bank paid me in the previous year. This was a very exciting concept for me since I was happy whenever I could buy a toy that cost a few dollars. I thought, *Wow! If I can just keep adding to my savings and earn free money every year, I could have A LOT of money one day!* Whether a kid or an adult, this mindset is all it takes to get rich.

The real value of the savings account wasn't the money that was deposited for me. It was the feeling it gave me. I felt like Peter Parker getting bitten by a radioactive spider and becoming Spider-Man. I may not be living a superhero's life, but it felt very exciting at the time, and it set me on a journey to discover how to build wealth.

Of course, the life of an aspiring superhero still has its challenges. I graduated from a good college with big dreams of getting a well-paying job. I ran into the reality of a job that barely paid the bills while living in a city with high rents. I quickly figured out that no one will pay you much when you are fresh out of college and they have to train you to do anything and everything. I decided to make life even more challenging when I quit my first job to move to another city with high rents to take an even *lower*-paying job just to work in a different industry and pursue a dream.

It was around that time that I started to read a few personal finance books and learn some basic strategies to build wealth and reduce my tax burden. Even though my salary was low and my tax burden was not great, I knew it was in my best interests to figure out ways to keep more of what I was earning. Maybe I became obsessed with it because I was earning so little money at the time.

I eventually worked my way up in the corporate world and entered a new realm of higher salaries and better benefits. Even though I took advantage of the ones that were relevant to me, I realized that many of my coworkers weren't. They were missing investment opportunities that could have helped them. This book is the result of years of living and working and investing in the real world and identifying the best opportunities available.

I know these lessons will provide some valuable insights to you on your journey, so let's get started!

PART 1

HOME RUN INVESTMENTS

Chapter 1

401(k) with an Employer Match

I am starting the first chapter with a bang: this is your chance to earn 100% on your investment if you work for an employer that offers a 401(k) with a good employer match. If you work for a government or nonprofit, you may have a similar plan called a 403(b). Even if you don't have a job like this yet, you'll probably have this option in the future. If you have ever turned down a job with a 401(k) match, you might want to rethink that decision when you consider what you may be missing out on.

What is a 401(k)?

A 401(k) is a special type of investment account that allows you to save for retirement. The money grows in a tax advantaged account, and you can begin to withdraw funds from the plan, penalty-free, at age 59½. I go into the details later, but for now, understand that you are putting away this money until you plan to retire. Virtually anyone with income can open some type of retirement account, but the employer match is what makes this special—and why I'm devoting an entire chapter to it.

What is the Employer Match?

Companies need to compete to recruit and retain good employees, so they want happy employees. A 401(k) with an employer match is one of the main programs employees use to save for retirement. The crazy thing is, millions of employees are not contributing to their employer-sponsored 401(k) plans; they are *turning down free money*. I hope this book changes that because a **401(k) with an employer match is an excellent home run investment.**

Employers may offer different levels of benefits. Some may offer no match at all, but typically, an employer may offer a 100% match on the first 3% of income that you contribute, then 50% on the next 2% you contribute. That means if you decide to invest 3% of your income, the employer will match with another 3%. That is a 100% return on your money. If you contribute 5% of your income, your employer will contribute 4%. If you contribute 6%, the employer will still contribute just 4%. A combined 10% of your income will go into the account when your 6% is combined with the employer's 4%.

Keep in mind that when I discuss the immediate profits on a home run investment, I am referring to the profit you make on new contributions. These profits will allow you to supercharge your savings. Once you capture these profits, you still need to decide what to invest in for your long-term plan. There are no guarantees on what you will earn on these investments in the future, but some investment options are discussed later in this book.

According to statistics from financial and investing advice company the Motley Fool, not everyone who's offered an employer-sponsored plan takes advantage of it; 79% of Americans can fund a 401(k), but only 41% of these workers opt to participate. As a result, just 32% of the total workforce is saving in a 401(k). This is a horribly low participation rate. This means that a large percentage of workers are not saving for retirement and are turning down free money. In a perfect world, the participation rate would be much closer to 100%, especially when the employer is offering to match an employee's contribution. These employees will never have such a good opportunity to build wealth so easily. Don't feel too bad if you are among those who have not taken advantage of a 401(k) plan. Hopefully, you will be ready to make some changes after you read this book.

If you are failing to plan, you are planning to fail. If you are not taking advantage of a 50% or 100% return on your money, you're making one of the biggest financial mistakes of your life. Remember how I mentioned that the world of Wall Street is focused on getting returns of 10% to 20% or more? This is your chance to beat all the

Wall Street bankers and make a big profit for yourself. Even if you are struggling to get by and paying off debt, you should at least make a contribution that allows you to get the full employer match and capture this free money.

Let's look at an example of a person that utilizes the employer match compared with a person that does not. In both situations, we will assume that this person earns $50,000 per year from age 25 to 65, gets a 2% raise every year, and the market goes up 8% annually, on average. Let's assume that Jane contributes 5% to her 401(k) and gets a 5% employer match, while Jim saves 5% in a similar account but with no employer match. The chart below shows the salaries for Jane and Jim, how much they are saving in their 401(k) plans, where they end up at the end of each year, and after 40 years of working.

Age	Salary for Jane and Jim	401k Contribution for Jane and Jim	401k Employer Match for Jane	Jane's 401k Balance	Jim's 401k Balance without the match
25	$50,000	$2,500	$2,500	$5,000	$2,500
26	$51,000	$2,550	$2,550	$10,500	$5,250
27	$52,020	$2,601	$2,601	$16,542	$8,271
28	$53,060	$2,653	$2,653	$23,171	$11,586
29	$54,122	$2,706	$2,706	$30,437	$15,219
30	$55,204	$2,760	$2,760	$38,393	$19,196
31	$56,308	$2,815	$2,815	$47,095	$23,547
32	$57,434	$2,872	$2,872	$56,606	$28,303
33	$58,583	$2,929	$2,929	$66,993	$33,496
34	$59,755	$2,988	$2,988	$78,328	$39,164
35	$60,950	$3,047	$3,047	$90,689	$45,344
36	$62,169	$3,108	$3,108	$104,161	$52,080
37	$63,412	$3,171	$3,171	$118,835	$59,417
38	$64,680	$3,234	$3,234	$134,810	$67,405
39	$65,974	$3,299	$3,299	$152,192	$76,096
40	$67,293	$3,365	$3,365	$171,096	$85,548
41	$68,639	$3,432	$3,432	$191,648	$95,824
42	$70,012	$3,501	$3,501	$213,981	$106,991
43	$71,412	$3,571	$3,571	$238,241	$119,120
44	$72,841	$3,642	$3,642	$264,584	$132,292
45	$74,297	$3,715	$3,715	$293,181	$146,590
46	$75,783	$3,789	$3,789	$324,213	$162,107
47	$77,299	$3,865	$3,865	$357,880	$178,940
48	$78,845	$3,942	$3,942	$394,395	$197,198
49	$80,422	$4,021	$4,021	$433,989	$216,995
50	$82,030	$4,102	$4,102	$476,911	$238,456
51	$83,671	$4,184	$4,184	$523,431	$261,716
52	$85,344	$4,267	$4,267	$573,840	$286,920
53	$87,051	$4,353	$4,353	$628,453	$314,226
54	$88,792	$4,440	$4,440	$687,608	$343,804
55	$90,568	$4,528	$4,528	$751,673	$375,837
56	$92,379	$4,619	$4,619	$821,045	$410,523
57	$94,227	$4,711	$4,711	$896,152	$448,076
58	$96,112	$4,806	$4,806	$977,455	$488,727
59	$98,034	$4,902	$4,902	$1,065,455	$532,727
60	$99,994	$5,000	$5,000	$1,160,690	$580,345
61	$101,994	$5,100	$5,100	$1,263,745	$631,873
62	$104,034	$5,202	$5,202	$1,375,248	$687,624
63	$106,115	$5,306	$5,306	$1,495,879	$747,940
64	$108,237	$5,412	$5,412	$1,626,373	$813,187
65	$110,402	$5,520	$5,520	$1,767,524	$883,762

At the end of 40 years, Jane has twice the amount in savings—an extra $883,762! As you can see, the employer match makes a huge difference to future savings. If you have a job without an employer match or you are self-employed, consider what this means. *And* we are just getting started; there is much more to come in terms of maximizing employee benefits and wealth-building opportunities.

Of course, you shouldn't feel compelled to work at a "regular" job if you're pursuing a dream that conflicts with a full-time job's schedule. However, you should at least be aware of what these benefits mean to you and your future if you're giving up a job with good benefits.

When you start a new job, you may have some kind of orientation meeting where a human resources person explains the 401(k), along with a few other benefits. But if you are new to the workforce or just aren't focused on these details, you could be missing out on some BIG opportunities. After you leave a job, you might maintain a few friendships and a few connections, but the money in your 401(k) will stay with you and it is a tangible reminder of your hard work.

Companies with 401(k) plans

Even if you don't think you have a strong background, the required education, or certain qualifications, you can likely still find a job with good benefits that include a 401(k) match. Many retailers and other companies that hire workers for entry-level work will give their employees opportunities to tap into these benefits. I have worked at some retail company headquarters and have always been impressed with the people that started off working in a store and stuck around long enough to get promoted and learn the business. You would be surprised how quickly you can rise through the ranks working at a chain store. Show up on time and work hard and ask your boss how you can move up, and you can be greatly rewarded. You could even end up working at the company headquarters or running the entire company. If this interests you, look up which big companies (including chain stores) are based in your hometown or home state. You might have opportunities closer to home than you realize.

Chain stores are just one example of where you might look for an entry-level job with good benefits. Internships, temporary jobs, and administration jobs will all give you a foot in the door and access to valuable benefits and wealth-creating opportunities.

Large companies are more likely to offer 401(k) plans and other benefits discussed in this book. Below are a few job types that can give you entry-level access to the corporate world:

- Bank teller

- Chef, waiter, or bartender (think about big chains like The Cheesecake Factory)
- Secretary or administrative assistant
- Coffee shop barista (consider chains like Starbucks)
- Flight attendant or another airline employee
- Grocery store employee
- Cell phone retailer
- Warehouse employee (Amazon and other e-commerce companies)

Here are a few big companies that are known to have reasonably good 401(k) plans for their employees at the time this book was written:

Walmart: Employees with a 401(k) plan through Walmart can get a dollar-for-dollar match up to a certain amount. The company matches any contribution of eligible wages up to 6% of pay.

Chick-fil-A: This plan ranks first among companies in the food services industry, according to a June 2019 study by *Money* magazine. All eligible, full-time Chick-fil-A employees can enroll in the 401(k), and the company matches up to 5%.

Costco: The company offers a 50% match for the first $1,000 in employee contributions each year, for a maximum employer match of $500 a year ($250 a year for West Coast Union employees).

Starbucks: The basic Starbucks 401(k) match is a 100% match on the first 4% of eligible pay that an employee contributes. If the company has a good year, Starbucks can also offer the "Enhanced Starbucks Match" with a 100% match on the first 6% of eligible pay.

Best Companies for a 401(k)

The list below is just a partial one and can change over time. Your best bet is to search for "companies with the best 401(k) plans" or look up a specific company you are interested in; they may have details on its website. You can also use GlassDoor.com or other company review websites to do some research. If you are focused on companies with great 401(k) plans, consider some of these as potential employers:

- Citigroup
- Google
- Apple
- Qualcomm
- Southwest Airlines
- UKG (Ultimate Kronos Group)
- Vimeo

More 401(k) tips

In 2022, the maximum amount workers can contribute to a 401(k) is $20,500. If you're age 50 and older, you can add an extra $6,500 per year in "catch-up" contributions, bringing your total 401(k) contributions for 2021 to $27,000.

If you can afford to contribute the maximum, go for it. If money is tight, at least take full advantage of the employer match. If you do contribute the maximum amount, make sure you don't contribute the maximum too early in the year; your employer may not be able to contribute matching funds later in the year.

Keep in mind that the earliest you can withdraw from your 401(k) without a penalty is age 59½. You should plan to leave the money in until then, if not longer. Regardless of what kind of 401(k) plan you use, it is critical to fully grasp the benefit of the free money in the employer match.

Pay Yourself First

The 401(k) benefit (and most of the benefits in this book) require you to "pay yourself first." This means planning what to do with your paycheck before the government, your landlord, your credit card company, or anyone else gets a cut of your earnings. If you prioritize your finances by paying yourself first and funneling your money to where you can make the best use of it, you will earn more money on your investments, reduce your tax expense, and still pay all your bills on time. The trick is to automate your savings and contributions.

This may require some short-term sacrifices in how much you spend on yourself and your family, but the long-term benefits are worth the extra effort. With a 401(k) plan, you are setting aside the money for years in the future. However, with many other savings programs in this book, you can access the money that you paid yourself in a few months.

401(k) Vesting

The vested balance in your 401(k) is the amount of money that belongs to you and cannot be taken back by an employer when you leave your job. Contributions that you make to your 401(k) are always fully vested. Vesting of employer contributions is based on a vesting schedule. When employer contributions to a 401(k) become vested, then the money is completely yours. Being fully vested means that the employer contributions will remain in your account even when you leave the company.

Whether an employer contribution is vested will depend on the type of contribution. "Safe harbor" matches are fully vested right away. Matching contributions that do not fall under the safe harbor provision and profit sharing contributions are usually subject to the company's vesting schedule. If you're not sure whether or when you will be fully vested, you should check with your employer. Make sure you understand what your employer offers and consider this if you are thinking about leaving your job before you are fully vested.

Understanding Early Withdrawals and Penalties

If you want to start a 401(k) but are nervous about locking the money up until you are much older, there are still ways to access the money under some special circumstances. You may be able to access some of the funds if you are willing to pay a 10% penalty on the withdrawal and applicable taxes. I don't recommend that you do this, and you should treat it as a last resort. However, I want to eliminate any excuse you may have for not starting a 401(k) and taking the free money that your employer offers. If you are turning down a 50% or 100% match today because you are worried about a 10% penalty down the road, you need to rethink your math. Open the account and take the money.

Be aware of the fine print if you think you may need to take an early 401(k) withdrawal at some point. Not every employer allows early withdrawals, so you will need to check with your human resources department to see if it is possible under some circumstances. If it is, you should still check the details of the plan to determine the type of withdrawals that are allowed.

The 401(k) Loan Option

Before taking an early withdrawal from your 401(k), find out if your plan allows you to take a loan against it since you can eventually replace the funds with this approach. You may also want to consider alternative options for securing financing that would hurt you less in the long run, such as a small personal loan.

The Hardship Withdrawal Option

You can also take something called a "hardship withdrawal" without a penalty. This is an option if you've encountered an economic hardship, are paying college tuition, or are funding a down payment for a first home. While you may be able to avoid a penalty, you would still pay income tax at your regular tax rate. You may also withdraw up to $5,000 penalty-free for a birth or adoption under the terms of the SECURE Act of 2019.

Final Disclaimer

Be sure to consult with a financial advisor if you are considering any of these options for a 401(k) so that you fully understand the potential risks and penalties.

Key Takeaways

A good 401(k) plan can give you an immediate
return of 50% to 100% on your investment.
Anytime someone is offering you free money,
you should take it!

Chapter 2

401(k) and IRA Tax Savings

As discussed in the first chapter, the 401(k) can provide an excellent return on investment if you have an employer match. A 401(k) offers another major benefit to you in the form of tax savings.

Taxes are a major topic in this book. If the government gives you a tax break for engaging in some type of investing or spending activity, it is the equivalent of a guaranteed rate of return in the year that you contribute. It is a home run investment. This is especially true if it is an activity you already were (or should have been) engaging in like saving and investing. For retirement planning, you are better off seeking a reduction in taxes with a 401(k) or IRA (Individual Retirement Account) than simply opening an investment account that has no special tax treatment.

The IRS is Your Frenemy

Nobody likes paying taxes. Most people do everything in their power to reduce what they pay because saving money on taxes means money back in your pocket. Unfortunately, many taxes—direct or indirect—are unavoidable. This includes sales tax, property tax, corporate tax, dividend tax, capital gains tax, payroll tax, state income tax, and federal income tax. The biggest expense over the course of your lifetime is likely to be taxes. For many people, it is bigger than housing or education or health care or any other expense.

Your federal income tax is usually the biggest tax liability you have. It is also the one where the government gives you the most flexibility to reduce your tax burden if you engage in certain activities that it encourages. This may include saving for retirement, paying for certain health care costs, buying a home, starting a business, or giving to charity.

The Internal Revenue Service (IRS) is the tax-collecting agency for the federal government. While the IRS is not your friend, it is also not quite your enemy; it is a frenemy—someone you are friendly with despite a fundamental dislike or rivalry. You probably have at least one frenemy in your personal life, like a relative, a close friend, an acquaintance, or even a coworker. Essentially, it's someone you like and hate at the same time.

The IRS is a lot like these frenemies. You may wish the IRS would just leave you alone, but it is inescapable and also gives you some benefits *if* you jump through the right hoops. However, if you don't pay attention to or take advantage of those hoops, you'll be fighting a losing battle.

Individual Retirement Accounts

An Individual Retirement Account (IRA) is a savings account with tax advantages similar to a 401(k) account. While the 401(k) plan is an employee benefit that can be obtained only through an employer, anyone who has earned income in a given year can open an IRA, including people who also have a 401(k). The only limitation is on the combined total they can contribute to retirement accounts in a single year while still getting tax advantages.

Traditional IRA

In most cases, contributions to traditional IRAs are tax-deductible. That is, if you put $6,000 into an IRA, your taxable income for the year decreases by that amount. However, when the money is withdrawn, it is taxed at your ordinary income tax rate. For 2022, annual individual contributions to traditional IRAs cannot exceed $6,000 in most cases. If you are 50 or older, you can contribute a total of up to $7,000 per year. Be aware that if your income is above a certain threshold, you may not be able to deduct your full IRA contribution.

If you plan to use an IRA, you may want to consult with an accountant to make sure you understand the tax implications of your situation.

What is the Tax Benefit?

Contributions to traditional 401(k) plans are made on a pretax basis, which removes them from your taxable income and reduces the taxes you'll pay for the year. So if you contribute $1,000, you don't have to pay taxes on this amount; if your highest tax bracket is 22%, you save $220 on your taxes. This is a huge benefit. In this example, the government is basically subsidizing you to make this investment to the tune of 22%. (Unfortunately, you don't get to reduce the taxes you pay into Social Security and Medicare, but we will discuss some examples of that later).

Let's take a minute to understand federal income tax brackets. Some people think that the more you make, the more you pay in taxes. This is true, but the government only taxes your income at a higher rate after they tax your first portion of income at a lower rate. We'll now examine actual tax brackets and some examples to make sure we understand the implications.

2022 Tax Rate	For Single Filers	For Married Individuals Filing Joint Returns	For Heads of Households
10%	$0 to $10,275	$0 to $20,550	$0 to $14,650
12%	$10,275 to $41,775	$20,550 to $83,550	$14,650 to $55,900
22%	$41,775 to $89,075	$83,550 to $178,150	$55,900 to $89,050
24%	$89,075 to $170,050	$178,150 to $340,100	$89,050 to $170,050
32%	$170,050 to $215,950	$340,100 to $431,900	$170,050 to $215,950
35%	$215,950 to $539,900	$431,900 to $647,850	$215,950 to $539,900
37%	$539,900 or more	$647,850 or more	$539,900 or more

If you make $50,000 per year, your highest marginal tax bracket is 22%. This percentage is the number you should use when considering the benefit of a tax deduction. If you make $250,000 per year, your highest marginal tax rate is 35%. The good news is that if you eventually go from making $50,000 to $250,000, not *all* of your income is taxed at 35%—only the amount you're making over $215,950. As you can see in the chart above, even when you are making much more money, you still pay just 10% on your first $10,275 of income. You pay 12% on earnings between $10,275 to $41,775, and on up the ladder. For simplicity, I will mostly use tax rates for people filing as single in this book, but the same principles are true for married people. Keep in mind that tax rates and employee benefits can change in the future but the principles in this book should still apply.

Traditional 401(k) Tax Savings

What are some examples of the immediate tax benefit of making a traditional 401(k) contribution? If you contribute $5,000 for the year and you are in the 22% tax bracket, that is an immediate tax savings of $1,100 for the year—going straight back into your pocket. You can use it to pay for groceries or set it aside to fund other types of investments. Suppose you contribute $10,000 and you are in the 35% tax bracket. You will get an immediate tax savings of $3,500 for the year. That is a great outcome for paying yourself first!

Capital Gains Tax

An additional tax benefit of a 401(k) is that you don't need to pay taxes on your profits each year. In a normal investment account not set up as an IRA or 401(k), the government taxes a piece of the profits you earned in dividends and capital gains. A capital gain is when you sell an investment for a profit. If you buy a stock or mutual fund for $10,000 and sell it for $20,000, then your capital gain is $10,000 and the government can tax this gain if it is not held in a 401(k) or IRA.

The capital gains tax rates on most assets held for under a year will correspond to your ordinary income tax brackets discussed above. Long-term capital gains tax rates apply to assets that are held for more than a year. These rates, shown below, are generally lower than your ordinary income tax rates.

Capital Gains Tax Rate	Single	Married Filing Separate	Head of Household	Married Filing Jointly
0%	$0 to $41,675	$0 to $41,675	$0 to $55,800	$0 to $83,350
15%	$41,675 to $459,750	$41,675 to $258,600	$55,800 to $488,500	$83,350 to $517,200
20%	$459,751 or more	$258,601 or more	$488,501 or more	$517,201 or more

If you make $50,000 in ordinary income and you have a long-term capital gain of $10,000, that gain is only taxed at 15% and you would owe $1,500 in taxes on that *capital gain*. That is better than paying 22% in *income taxes* on the gain.

Dividend Taxes

A dividend is like the interest you collect on a savings account. If you own stocks or mutual funds, the dividend is a form of profit-sharing where the shareholder collects a dividend for holding the stock. The tax rate on dividends is similar to the tax on capital gains. See the chart below.

Dividend Tax Rate	Single	Married Filing Separate	Head of Household	Married Filing Jointly
0%	$0 to $41,675	$0 to $41,675	$0 to $55,800	$0 to $83,350
15%	$41,676 to $459,750	$41,676 to $258,600	$55,801 to $488,500	$83,351 to $517,200
20%	$459,751 or more	$258,601 or more	$488,501 or more	$517,201 or more

Most dividends collected from stocks and mutual funds are paid as **qualified** dividends with the tax rates listed here. But be aware that some investments like REITs (Real Estate Investment Trusts) pay non-qualified dividends that are taxed as ordinary income. Because of this, it's usually a good idea to hold some assets in an IRA or 401(k) for better tax treatment.

Example of the Tax Benefit

Let's look at an example of two workers. Worker A makes $50,000 per year and invests $5,000 of his income in a 401(k) or IRA each year for 30 years. Worker B also makes $50,000 per year and invests $5,000 in a regular investment account and is required to pay taxes on his profits each year. For this example, we will ignore the potential benefit of an employer contribution to the 401(k) for Worker A. We will assume that both workers earn 8% each year on their investments and pay 22% in marginal taxes.

Worker A will accumulate $611,729 in a tax-advantaged account like a 401(k). It will be $510,149 after taxes on the earnings. Worker B accumulates only $438,129 in a taxable savings account.

The numbers get even more impressive if we make slightly different assumptions. Suppose the workers contribute $10,000 per year, earn 10% on their investments, and are in the 35% tax bracket. In a tax-deferred vehicle, Worker A would accumulate $1,809,434 ($1,281,132 after taxes on the earnings) versus Worker B's $919,892 in a taxable savings account.

You can experiment with different numbers with an online calculator. A simple one is at NewYorkLife.com

(https://www.newyorklife.com/learn-and-plan/tax-deferral-calculator).

Keep in mind that real-world results will vary based on actual stock market performance and your tax situation.

What Is the Catch with a 401(k)?

There *is* a catch with a traditional 401(k)—you will still be taxed after you retire and start to withdraw funds from the account.

Deposits to your 401(k) or IRA doesn't mean taxes were eliminated forever; they are just deferred. You will still owe money to the IRS in the future on any investment earnings from these savings accounts. Some people call this the "tax bomb."

When you withdraw funds from your 401(k) in retirement, it's called taking a "distribution." You will begin to pay taxes on this money since you previously invested this money without paying any taxes. For most people, and with most 401(k)s, distributions are taxed as ordinary income.

Figuring Out Your Taxes on a Traditional 401(k)

Distributions from a traditional 401(k) are simple in terms of tax treatment: Your contributions to the plan were paid with pretax dollars, which means they reduced your taxable earned income, and subsequently reduced the income taxes you paid *at that time*. Because of that deferral, taxes are due on the 401(k) funds once the distributions begin in retirement. The distributions from these plans are taxed as ordinary income at the rate for your tax bracket in the year you make the withdrawal.

The Roth 401(k) and Roth IRA

You may also have the choice to invest your money into a Roth 401(k) if your employer offers it. If your employer does not offer it, consider putting some money into a Roth IRA.

If you put money into a Roth 401(k) or Roth IRA, you will not receive a reduction in your taxes when you contribute. Instead, you will make the contribution with "after-tax" dollars; when you retire, you will not have to pay any taxes on the distributions from your account. Imagine paying no taxes on your investment in the future! That can be a great deal for most people.

Roth 401(k) Versus Traditional 401(k)

Which 401(k) should you choose? Give serious consideration to a Roth 401(k) or Roth IRA because if you do everything I recommend, hopefully, you will retire rich. The only downside to retiring rich is that you will probably be in a higher tax bracket. This is not for certain, however, and is one of the most frustrating things about deciding between a Roth 401(k) or a traditional 401(k). You don't know what the tax rates will be in the future AND you don't know what your income will be when you retire. Here are just a few reasons you could end up retiring with a much higher income than you have today:

- The stock market goes up dramatically in the next 20 to 30 years and makes you much richer

- You own shares of your employer's stock and the stock goes up significantly

- You receive an inheritance

- Your house increases in value and you sell it, giving you new investment income

- You start a new business or create some other stream of income

I want you to plan with an abundance mentality and expect to have a lot of money (which might be taxable income) when you retire. Even if you never make more than $60,000 per year in your working life, you could still retire rich if you save diligently and follow the advice in this book.

Having much more money flowing into your bank account in retirement than ever before could put you in a higher tax bracket—you could be paying 35% or more on your income. Most experts anticipate taxes will go up for nearly everyone in the future, especially high-income individuals. Income taxes could easily shoot up to 50% or more. Before the tax reforms of the 1980s, the federal income tax rate was 55% on income above $41,500, and it was 70% on income above $108,300.

To put that in context, the dollar was much stronger then and the government offered more tax deductions that allowed people to reduce their taxable income. The point is that tax rates could easily return to those levels in the future if the government feels compelled to make a significant change to the tax code to pay for future government expenses. It would not be unprecedented. These types of higher tax rates are common in Europe, where even middle-class people pay much higher tax rates than what we have in America.

Additionally, there's no guarantee that the government will *never* tax the Roth 401(k) and Roth IRA accounts. While laws could change, most experts believe that it would be too unpopular to tax Roth accounts because they are held by millions of voters that already paid taxes on this money and have made plans assuming they will *not* be taxed again. There could be a taxpayer revolt if the government tries to tax Roth accounts.

The message here is to choose a 401(k) option with your eyes open and think about taxes in all your financial decisions; you could also diversify your long-term tax strategy and use both a Roth plan and a traditional plan. Just make sure you don't contribute more than the amount allowed. Again, you may want to consult with an accountant about your situation and income level. Now, go out and get that employer match and plan for an amazing future.

Key Takeaways

A 401(k) and an IRA can help you to save a significant amount of money on taxes over time. Do whatever you legally can to reduce your taxes and you will end up with significantly more wealth.

Chapter 3

Employee Stock Purchase Plans

If you work for a company that has publicly traded stock, there is a good chance that your employer offers an employee stock purchase plan (ESPP). If you don't work for a company like this, consider it as a potential benefit in a future job.

An ESPP allows employees to buy the company stock at a discounted rate—often, 15% off the regular price. That means if the company stock is $100 per share you can buy it at $85 per share. If someone was handing out $100 bills and you could buy them for $85, would you do it? *Yes*. It is an amazing deal—and in most cases, it's a home run investment! There are few places where you can get a quick 15% return on your investment with such little risk.

Not Enough People Are Using ESPPs

We've already established that there is a huge problem and missed opportunity for millions of Americans who aren't saving and investing enough. The same problem holds true for ESPPs. Most publicly traded companies offer ESPPs, but participation rates are stubbornly low.

In a 2018 Deloitte survey on companies with ESPPs, 67% of respondents said they offer a share purchase discount of 15%, while 27% offer a discount that is less than 15%. 6% of companies offer a discount greater than 15%.

In the same study, 37% of companies report a participation rate of less than 25% by their eligible employees. Only 10% of companies had a participation rate above 75%. In a perfect world, that number would be reversed and we would see 90% of companies with a participation rate above 75%.

I remember vividly asking one of my coworkers if he was selling all of his stock in the ESPP. He said he didn't participate because he didn't like to tie up this extra money. I was shocked. In fact, that conversation was part of the inspiration for this book. This highly intelligent, educated person was *turning down free money*. It was a total mystery to me as to why. However, I suspect he was thinking about the ESPP profit in terms of dollars each quarter and failing to consider the percentage profit he could make each year. There is no other place he could make such a big profit with such a low risk.

How the ESPP Works

With an ESPP, your employer allows you to contribute some portion of your income to buying company stock. The maximum is usually 10% of your income, and you should try your best to contribute the maximum amount allowed—assuming it meets the basic criteria discussed in this chapter.

In most cases, you contribute to the stock purchase program in each pay period, and then once per quarter, that money is used to buy the stock and is deposited into an account for you. Usually, there is no obligation to hold onto the stock; you can turn around and sell the stock right away on the day you get it. I generally recommend that you sell the stock right away because there is no need to take on the potential risk associated with the company stock. When you sell the stock it converts back to cash, and you can spend it on your everyday needs or other investments.

If you believe strongly in the company, you might consider keeping the stock or just selling half. You could also just sell enough to recoup your investment and leave the rest of your profit in the stock. It is totally up to you, but it's important to understand that you are taking some risk if you hold onto the stock.

ESPP Taxes

If you sell your ESPP shares right away, the profit will usually be taxed as ordinary income. If you are in the 22% tax bracket, you will pay 22% of the profit in taxes. If you sell after holding the stock for a year, profits may be taxed at a lower rate as long-term capital gains.

Every company can have a slightly different policy for its ESPP. It is best to consult your HR or benefits departments for details specific to your company. You can consult with an accountant or financial advisor if you plan to hold onto the stock since this could change the taxes you eventually pay on it. If you choose to hold onto your ESPP shares, it could put you in an overexposed position—if the stock value decreases, you may lose money on the stock; if the company does very poorly, you could lose your job too.

Example of a Stock Purchase

Let's say Tina makes $60,000 per year. Her employer allows her to contribute 10% of her income to the stock plan. This means every three months she earns $15,000 and contributes $1,500 to the stock. At the end of the quarter, the money is used to buy the stock at a 15% discount; Tina will have $1,765 in stock based on the 15% discount. The dollar gain is $265—a 17.6% return on her initial investment.

And this 17.6% is just the return you get for a *three-month period*. If you make this $265 profit four times a year, that is a total profit of $1,060. If you are just reusing the same $1,500 that you have set aside for this purpose every quarter, you are effectively earning a profit of 70.4% on your money for the year! That is an amazing profit for setting aside $1,500 every three months.

Is There a Risk?

The main risk in the example above is that on the day you receive the stock in your account, the stock price could fall. Of course, it could jump up in value just as easily. The odds are very low that it will fall by more than the amount of the discount and the odds that this would happen repeatedly over several quarters or several years are even lower. Just make sure you understand any potential restrictions in your employer's plan.

Lookback Provisions—Even More Profit for You!

While many ESPPs offer a standard 15% discount, some plans allow for something called a "lookback" provision. This allows an ESPP to purchase shares of stock at the purchase date price or the grant date price, whichever is lower. The grant date price is usually the price of the stock on the date when the offering period began.

If the grant date price for your ESPP shares was $100 per share and the purchase date price was $150 per share, you will get an even bigger profit. If you were able to contribute $1,250 to the plan, your stock would be worth $1,875 when the stock is deposited in your account. That is a $625 profit to you, and a 50% profit based on your investment.

What If I Can't Afford to Contribute to the ESPP?

I highly recommend you find a way to fund your ESPP contribution. Remember, you will generally get your money back in three or four months, depending on the type of program your employer has. If necessary, you can cut back on some expenses. You could explain the program to a friend or relative to get a short-term loan. You could also use your credit cards to cover some extra expenses for a few months and then pay off the debt as soon as you sell the stock.

You can also look into a company such as Carver Edison. They provide short-term loans so you can increase your contribution to the stock purchase plan. After you receive the stock, Carver Edison receives some shares to reimburse them for the loan. Your net shares are then deposited into your brokerage account. The specifics of this plan could change over time. Carver Edison works directly with companies, so your company would need to be working with them to participate in this type of loan. If this is an option, be sure to do your homework and understand any costs associated with the offer. I encourage you to buy the stock without any help if you can. But I also want to rid you of any excuse you may have for not participating in the plan.

Review the company's ESPP document in detail. You can also consult an accountant to fully understand the tax consequences of the plan. However, don't let the specific tax rate dissuade you. If you can earn 15% or more on your money for such a small risk, you should absolutely take advantage of the plan. The same is true even if the employer is offering just a 5% discount. Take advantage of it and squeeze everything you can out of this benefit.

Key Takeaways

Many ESPP programs allow you to get a quick 15% return on your investment. Usually, this is done quarterly so you can get this profit four times per year. This is an excellent return on your investment.

Chapter 4

Health Care Flexible Spending Accounts

Let's continue along the journey of maximizing your employee benefits and reducing your taxes. If possible, you should take full advantage of a health care flexible spending account (HCFSA or FSA). An FSA is generally only available as part of an employee benefits package. It can be very rewarding because FSA accounts allow you to use pretax dollars to pay out-of-pocket medical expenses. You can use the money in your FSA for medical copayments and deductibles, as well as some other covered medical and dental expenses. It includes things like:

- Prescription medications
- Some over-the-counter medicines
- Medical supplies like bandages
- Medical equipment like crutches
- Many other health care-related items

If your employer offers an FSA, you can enroll with your benefits department and determine how much you want to put into the fund. The maximum amount you can put into an FSA in 2022 is $2,850. When you participate in this benefit, your employer deducts an amount from each paycheck to fund it. This means that you will reduce your taxable income by whatever you put into the FSA.

Let's take a closer look at your taxes. Taxes on your paycheck can include 22% in federal income tax, as well as an **additional 6.2% in Social Security tax and 1.45% in Medicare tax**. When you add these up, you are paying **approximately 30% in tax** on your earnings. The Social Security tax of 6.2% applies to the first $147,000 of your income in 2022. You do not pay the Social Security tax on earnings above that level.

If you contribute the maximum amount of $2,850 and you save 30% in taxes on that amount, you will save $825 for the year. That is extra money in your pocket that you can spend or invest because you planned ahead and took advantage of this benefit. The FSA benefit reduces your income taxes along with your payroll taxes—so even if you are in the 22% income tax bracket, the total savings would be about 30%.

I hope you're seeing a theme here: you should always think about taxes when making investment and spending decisions. Anytime you can reduce your taxes and save 22 to 30%, it's the equivalent of getting a 22 or 30% return on investment. Those opportunities simply don't exist out in the investment world—so take advantage of these home run investments whenever your employer and the government are trying to assist you.

I remember when I first heard about the HCFSA benefit. Before I was married, I had virtually no health care bills—no doctor visits, no prescription drugs. I couldn't think of any routine "health care" costs, so I didn't sign up for it. It wasn't until later that I realized I could have signed up and used the money for my contact lenses, new eyeglasses, bandages, neti pots, and everything else in an online FSA store. I could have gotten a pretax deduction on many expenses, and I missed it—because no one told me it was for more than just doctor visits! And that's why I'm telling you now. Be sure to sign up if you know you will have some eligible expenses.

There *Is* a Catch

The FSA is not a normal savings account. It is a benefit designed to finance your annual out-of-pocket medical expenses. You can lose whatever amount is left unspent in the account at the end of the year. However, the IRS offers employers the ability to let employees use up any extra FSA funds from the prior year until March 15 of the following year. The IRS also allows employers to let their employees roll forward up to $500 in unspent FSA funds into the next year. Be sure to check your company's policy to find out whether they take advantage of this option.

Because there is some risk of losing money that you put into the FSA, try to plan out your health care spending ahead of time if you can. If you anticipate a big medical bill that will not be fully covered by insurance, you might contribute the maximum amount. If you have very little in health care spending, you might put in a small amount just to cover your basics.

Keep in mind that you can also use any extra money to stock up on things that you will need in the future. Check out FSAstore.com for ideas on where you can spend your money. Everything on the site is eligible for use with your FSA. Amazon also has an FSA store where you can browse and spend your tax-free dollars. Additional products include eyeglasses, contact lenses, thermometers, cold and allergy medicines, headache and pain medicine, bandages and first aid kits, some lotions, and much more.

Nothing is stopping you from spending hundreds of dollars on essentials that you will need to use in the future if you have surplus money in your FSA. If you are mindful of your spending, your FSA is a home run investment!

Key Takeaways

A health care FSA is an excellent way to reduce your taxes if your employer offers this benefit. You can use it for most of your health care expenses so be sure to exploit this opportunity where you can.

Chapter 5

Dependent Care Flexible Spending Account

A dependent care FSA (DCFSA) is a pretax benefit account used to pay for eligible dependent care services, such as day care, summer day camp, before or after school programs, and child care for children under the age of 13. It works in much the same way as a health care FSA, but the money is specifically for another person's needs.

You can contribute up to $5,000 in 2022 if you are married filing jointly or are a single parent. If you have a child in day care or pay any type of nanny, it is likely that you will easily use up the $5,000. If you are married and filing separately, you may contribute up to $2,500. (In some cases, your employer could choose a lower contribution limit).

Using this benefit will, once again, reduce your taxes. The funds are withdrawn from your paycheck and you do not pay Medicare and Social Security payroll taxes on the money. If you are in the 22% tax bracket, again, you will save nearly 30% on the money you funnel through this account.

The main types of expenses that qualify are:

- Care for your child who is less than 13 years old

- After school care and before school care

- Nanny and babysitting expenses

- Daycare and nursery school

- Summer day camp

- Care for your spouse or a relative who is physically or mentally incapable of self-care and lives in your home

Use It or Lose It

Any money you contribute to a dependent care FSA must be used up that year or forfeited. A dependent care FSA plan allows a reasonable time for employees to submit claims after the end of the year, but all dependent care expenses must be incurred by the end of the year.

If you have any questions about whether your care provider qualifies for the FSA plan, be sure to talk with your human resources department or the company administering the plan. You should also verify if you and your spouse are eligible for the plan. If your spouse does not have any earned income, you might not be eligible for the benefit. If you can capture the tax savings it will be a home run investment for you.

Key Takeaways

A dependent care FSA is an excellent way to reduce your taxes if your employer offers this benefit. It is similar to a health care FSA, but you can get an even bigger potential tax benefit every year that you are eligible for the benefit.

Chapter 6

Health Savings Accounts

If you are looking for more ways to build wealth and reduce your taxes, explore the possibility of using a health savings account. This differs from a health care FSA, as I'll explain. Your employer may also offer an HSA as part of your health insurance options. While I outline the HSA's financial benefits in this chapter, I recommend that you research all the health insurance plans that are available to you.

HSAs are tax-advantaged savings accounts designed to help people who have high-deductible health plans (HDHPs) pay for out-of-pocket medical expenses. Relatively few Americans take advantage of these types of accounts, even though more than 40% of employers currently offer them. According to a 2020 *Journal of the American Medical Association* study, 55% of people with HSA's don't contribute to them. Most employees who are eligible for HSAs have been missing out on a great option for building wealth.

The HSA and health care FSA both offer pretax savings for eligible healthcare expenses and can both be a part of an employee benefits package. However, HSAs are quite different in certain respects; HSAs require a high-deductible health insurance plan, and self-employed individuals are eligible. HSAs have higher contribution limits and unused funds roll over at the end of the year.

High-Deductible Health Plans

To decide whether you want an HSA, first decide if you want or need a high-deductible health insurance plan. A high-deductible plan typically means that you save money on your monthly insurance premiums, but you pay more out of pocket when you need to see a doctor or use your insurance for other health care needs. Depending on your health care costs for a given year, you could end up saving (or spending) more money with a high-deductible plan.

An HDHP may be advantageous if you are healthy and rarely get sick or injured. Consider whether you can afford to pay your deductible right away if you are hit with an unexpected medical expense. The HDHP may be beneficial if you have the means to make significant contributions to an HSA each month.

You may decide you want a more conventional low-deductible plan since it makes health expenses easier to predict, even though you will have higher monthly premiums. A low-deductible plan may be better if you are pregnant, planning to become pregnant, or have children. You may save money with these plans if you have a chronic condition, are considering surgery—such as a knee or hip replacement—or if you take some expensive prescription medications. You should also consider injuries that you or your family may get from playing certain sports.

Why Use an HSA for Retirement?

An HSA's tax-advantaged status, similar to that of a traditional 401(k) plan or IRA, makes it a powerful way to save for retirement. It may be the best way to save for retirement medical expenses. The HSA has a **triple tax advantage**. First, you make contributions with pretax dollars. Second, you get to grow your savings every year without paying any taxes on the investment. Third, you can withdraw the money in retirement without paying any taxes if you use the with-drawals for qualified medical expenses. You can also use the money for non-medical expenses when you're retired, but the withdrawals will be taxed the same way that a traditional IRA withdrawal is taxed.

HSA contributions are tax-deductible even if you do not itemize, and can be deducted via payroll. You can even pay out of pocket; if you do, they are made on a pretax basis. It can reduce your federal and state income tax liability, and the contributions are not subject to FICA taxes (Social Security and Medicare). That means if you are in the 22% tax bracket, you will actually save 30% when you contribute.

Your account balance grows tax-free, so any dividends or capital gains you earn are not taxable. If your employer makes contributions to your HSA, this does not have to be counted as part of your taxable income.

Withdrawals for qualified medical expenses are completely tax-free as well—the tax treatment on the HSA is even better than the tax treatment on a traditional 401(k) or IRA. Once you begin to withdraw funds from a traditional retirement plan, you pay income tax on that money, no matter how you use it. (With a Roth IRA, you withdraw the money tax-free in retirement but you paid into it with after-tax dollars). An HSA allows you to make contributions with pretax dollars, and then you never pay taxes on the money you spend at all if used on acceptable purchases.

Additionally, the HSA does not require the account holder to begin withdrawing funds at a certain age; the account can remain untouched as long as you want. However, be aware that you are not allowed to contribute once you enroll in Medicare (typically at age 65).

You can carry the balance from year to year. You are not required to spend it every year as with an FSA, which operates under a "use it or lose it" system. An HSA can even move with you to a new job because it is fully portable.

How to Get an HSA

To qualify for an HSA, you must have a high-deductible health plan and no other health insurance coverage. You must not yet qualify for Medicare. Also, you cannot be claimed as a dependent on someone else's tax return.

For 2022, the deductible for an HDHP is at least $1,400 for an individual's coverage and $2,800 for family coverage. Depending on your coverage, your annual out-of-pocket expenses in 2022 could run as high as $7,050 for individual coverage—or $14,100 for family coverage—under an HDHP. As I have noted, there is some risk here, and so these plans are usually more popular with affluent people who will benefit from the tax advantages and can afford the risk.

However, a lower-deductible plan can still cost you more than $2,000 a year in higher premiums. You pay this extra money regardless of the amount of your medical expenses in a given year. With an HDHP, your spending is more in line with your actual healthcare needs. Again, individual needs vary, so consider your circumstances. You can contribute up to the maximum amount to an HSA regardless of your income, even if you are self-employed, and even if you have no income. The contribution limit for a family health savings account in 2022 is $7,300; $3,650 for an individual HSA.

Employer Contributions

Some employers will make contributions to your HSA. The average annual employer contribution for HSAs is around $600 for individual employees and $1,250 for employee family plans. According to the Employee Benefit Research Institute, about two-thirds of employees reported that their employers contributed to the account. If your employer is willing to contribute to your account, it will increase your wealth-building potential and make it an even better investment for you. Check with your employer to see if they will contribute to your account.

Should You Spend Your Contributions?

This chapter covers how to use the HSA as an investment tool. The main idea for an HSA is to give people with a high-deductible health plan a tax break to make their out-of-pocket medical expenses more manageable. However, the special tax advantage means that the ideal way to use an HSA is to treat it as an investment tool. The best way to build up this wealth is to minimize any withdrawals from your HSA for medical bills and just pay cash if you can afford to. You can also use money from your FSA in some limited circumstances, but in most cases, you cannot use both an FSA and HSA.

Think of your HSA contributions the same way you think of your contributions to a retirement account. The goal is to contribute money and watch it grow as much as possible. If you do need to spend some of the funds in your HSA, be sure to spend them on qualified medical expenses. If you are forced to spend it on anything else before you turn 65, you will face a 20% penalty and have to pay income tax on those funds.

Investment Choices

The key to maximizing your HSA is to invest the money in something that will grow over time. Look at the details of your specific plan. Your general goal should be similar to your other investment goals. Consider investing some of the money in a fund that functions like an S&P 500 index fund. We will discuss index funds later in this book.

Your employer might open the HSA with a particular administrator, but you can choose where to put your money. Don't just leave it in a savings account. Look for simple low-cost index funds; Vanguard and Fidelity typically offer good options for this.

Building Wealth

Let's look at an example of how well the HSA savings and investment strategy can turn out for you. Assume you are currently 21 and you make the maximum contribution of $3,600 every year to an individual-only plan until you are 65. Let's also assume that all the money is invested in a stock market index fund that earns an average annual return of 8%. By age 65, your HSA would be worth more than $1.2 million!

State Taxes

Most states allow you to deduct the HSA contributions from your state income tax, but not all. Check your state tax laws and make your financial calculations accordingly.

Your Final Decision on the HSA

As you evaluate the HSA option, you must first decide whether you are comfortable with a high-deductible health care plan. If it is a good choice for you and your family, try to participate in the HSA.

We have covered a lot of ground here, but the key thing to remember here is that your HSA is another potential home run investment. Even if you only make small contributions to this account, you will receive an immediate tax benefit. In theory, you can leave your contributions in cash after you capture this short-term benefit. It is up to you to decide what to invest in after making the contributions. To capture the benefits of future compounding interest, pick some investments and accept the risks associated with them.

If you are in the 22% tax bracket, your total savings is nearly 30% when you include savings from payroll taxes. If you don't use the HSA as an investment vehicle, you can still save money on your taxes right away by making the contributions, even if you do spend the money on medical bills. As you know by now, a 30% return on your investment is excellent—whether it comes from tax savings or a profit on an investment.

Key Takeaways

A Health Savings Account can be a great opportunity to build wealth if you are comfortable with a high-deductible health plan. You make contributions with pretax dollars, the money grows tax-free every year, and you can withdraw it for qualified medical expenses without paying any tax. This is one of the best possible investments from a tax perspective.

Chapter 7

Commuter Benefits

We have covered some of the most common employee benefits that allow you to save money on your taxes and build wealth. Your employer may offer even *more* benefits, including a tax benefit for commuters. This chapter includes a summary of some additional benefits you should look for. Talk to your human resources department (or senior executives) and push them to add additional benefits. In one of my previous jobs, I did this successfully, and by adding just one new benefit, employees saved thousands of dollars. Some employers will also reduce their tax obligations if they offer certain benefits.

Qualified Transportation Fringe Benefits (QTF)

Another tax-free benefit that may be available to you through your employer is called a qualified transportation fringe (QTF) benefit. This benefit can be used to pay for certain qualified transportation expenses including:

- A ride in a commuter highway vehicle between home and the workplace

- A transit pass

- Qualified parking

A *commuter highway vehicle* seats at least six adults, excluding the driver. At least 80% of the mileage must be for transporting employees between home and work, and at least half of the passenger seats must be for employees.

A *transit pass* is a token, fare card, voucher, etc., that entitles someone to ride free or at a reduced rate on public transit or a vehicle for hire with seats for at least six adults. In some cases, the cost is deducted via payroll and delivered directly to the employee in the form of a public transit pass or voucher.

Qualified parking is reserved by a company for employees near the office or public transit, commuter highway vehicles, or carpools. It does not include parking at the employee's home.

In 2022, the maximum tax-free benefit is $280 per month, totaling $3,360 for the year. This benefit reduces your Social Security and Medicare taxes—so if you are in the 22% income tax bracket, you will save 30% on this home run investment. If you save 30% on $3,360, then $996 goes back into your pocket.

More Benefits

If you work for a large, fast-growing company, there may be other benefits. Some big companies like Google and Apple can offer things like student loan repayment. I trust that if you work for a company like this and you can sign up for something as generous as student loan repayment, you will do so. It is essentially free money and may not necessarily require a payroll deduction or short-term reduction in your pay.

Paychecks and Profits

You may be wondering if you can take advantage of all these deductions and benefits. They may require some short-term sacrifice to achieve financial gain. Before I got my first corporate job, I talked to a friend that had a job with good benefits. He told me his goal was to reduce his take-home pay to the smallest possible amount and just live off that. I was confused when he first said this. Why would you want to take home *less money* in each paycheck? He explained that it meant he was living below his means, a good thing. He started to explain some of the specific benefit programs in this book. He was maximizing his 401(k) contributions and buying discounted stock through an ESPP. He was taking advantage of other benefits that resulted in a short-term expense but a long-term benefit.

If you earn $120,000 annually, that is $10,000 every month. But of course, you don't have $10,000 to spend each month. Even under the best of circumstances, you'll have to pay a large portion of that in taxes and health insurance premiums and other deductions. When you think about what you earn, it is best to focus on your *net* pay and not your *gross* pay when planning your weekly and monthly expenses. It also helps to limit any wasteful splurges on things you don't really need.

Think of your paycheck as a profit center. Your company is paying you for your labor, so that is one type of profit. But if you can take advantage of some or all of these benefits and tax incentives, you can create another layer of profit for yourself. You just need to plan accordingly and spend some time to understand your **paychecks and profits**.

The 401(k) is the only benefit I've outlined here that is truly locked up until retirement. (And even then, you can access some of that money in an emergency if you are prepared to pay a penalty). The ESPP, FSA, HSA, and QTF programs allow you to funnel money into special accounts for just a few months at a time, and in most cases, you will still have access to that money in the same year that you contributed.

I recommend you figure out a way to live below your means and maximize your savings. If you are having trouble with this, consider that you can still come out ahead even if you have to rely on some temporary, increased credit card spending to make sure you are maximizing your long-term wealth and reducing your taxes. Even if you pay 20% interest on your credit card, you are better off living off the credit card for a few months if that is what it takes to participate in a discounted stock offering or a program that can reduce your taxes. If you put an extra $1,000 on your credit card and you have to pay approximately 1.8% interest that month, that is only $18 in interest payments a month (assuming you are not getting hit with late fees or other penalties).

If you already own a home, you might be able to tap into a HELOC (home equity line of credit) to help with a short-term need for extra cash. Your bank may have other types of loan programs with better interest rates than what credit card companies are offering. (There is an entire chapter devoted to credit cards; be sure to read that chapter carefully and proceed with caution if you plan to use your credit cards to cover some short-term expenses).

Most of these benefits and deductions will allow you to recapture the money in just a few months. If you're able to make your credit card interest payments and avoid any late fees and penalties, you should be able to pay off any extra debt very quickly and will likely not need to pay a full year of credit card interest expense. Plus, you can shop around for a lower interest credit card and transfer the balance to a new one if that is what it takes.

Obviously, this should not be an excuse to spend more than you usually do. It is just a way to borrow a bit of money to make some smart investments. Businesses and entrepreneurs use short-term borrowing to finance profitable investments all the time. On Wall Street, they sometimes call this arbitrage. If you can borrow money at 10% and make a 20% profit with virtually no risk, that is arbitrage. Fortunes are made this way.

Tax Refunds

Most employees pay a significant amount of money in federal income tax. You set your tax withholding based on what you earn and what you think you will owe when you file a tax return by April 15. While most people are excited if they get a tax refund, it really means they paid more than they needed to during the year. They could have reduced their withholding and had more money in their pocket all year to spend or invest. In effect, they gave the government an interest-free loan.

If you are routinely getting a refund on your tax return, consider adjusting the W-4 withholdings you claimed with your employer so that you pay a bit less income tax on each paycheck. You can use the IRS online "Tax Withholding Estimator" and input the details of your income to make sure you are withholding the right amount. This could free up some money for you to participate in the programs in this book. You can update your withholdings anytime you want to.

Ultimately, we all need to learn to live below our means. The world is filled with examples of famous athletes, musicians, and other entertainers who made millions of dollars over a short period and ended up filing for bankruptcy when the income slowed down because they never learned to save, invest, and live on less than what they earned. Even lottery winners have managed to blow through millions of dollars in prize money and end up broke. Learn from their mistakes and start by maximizing your savings and home run investments now.

Key Takeaways

Look for ways to reduce taxes and maximize your benefits whenever you can. Find a way to make short-term sacrifices to profit from these investments. I have shown you the way. No excuses!

Chapter 8

Credit Cards

My eight-year-old son seems to think that credit cards are like magic. Whenever I mention we need to buy or save for something, he says, "Just put it on your credit card and the credit card company will pay for it." I always tell him the same thing in response. "We still pay for everything. The credit card just makes the payment a little faster and easier than using cash." Some adults didn't get this message when they were kids.

Do you have high-interest credit card debt? If so, do everything you can to pay it off quickly. This is effectively a home run investment. It's technically not an *investment* like a savings account or an investment asset, but whenever you allocate money to different categories, think about the rate of return on that money. Think in terms of percentages.

Many people have credit card debt that requires them to pay 20% or more on that loan. If you can eliminate that debt, you are effectively getting a 20% return on your money risk-free. If you have $1,000 in a savings account, it may only earn 1% per year, earning you $10 per year. However, if you have $1,000 in credit card debt and the credit card company is charging you 20% interest, you're losing $200 per year. Eliminating $200 per year in interest payments is the equivalent of finding an investment that pays you 20%, risk-free.

That 20% interest rate is costing you more than $200 per year in this example because you pay the debt with after-tax dollars. If you are paying 22% income tax, that means you need to earn $256 at your job just to have $200 in after-tax income to pay that interest. Actually, it's even worse than *that*. As I mentioned previously, taxes on your paycheck include 22% in federal income tax, as well as an additional 6.2% in Social Security tax and 1.45% in Medicare tax. When you add these up, you are paying nearly 30% in tax on your earnings. It's even more if you live in a state with a state income tax, but we will ignore that for now.

Based on the tax rate of 30%, that $1,000 of debt is costing you $284 in terms of what you need to earn to pay the $200 of interest on the debt. When you pay it off completely, it is the equivalent of a 28.4% return. This is an excellent "investment" with zero risk. Manage your credit card bill as if it were an investment that puts money back in your pocket. Even if you are paying 10% or less on your credit card debt, the same principle still holds. Paying it off quickly gives you an excellent return on your money; one you cannot easily find in other investments.

If you can pay it all off now with savings, you should probably do it. You can see how the average person can get trapped into a large amount of credit card debt with high interest payments. Even if you work hard at your job, you will be paying credit card interest with after-tax dollars—meaning the government taxes roughly 30% of what you earn, leaving you to try and catch up on your bills with the leftover money. It's not easy! That is why you should avoid debt and reduce your taxes whenever possible so that you have more money left in your bank account to invest and spend.

Struggling with Credit Card Debt

This book focuses a great deal on compound interest. This means you invest, then you make a profit, and you continue to make profits on the profits. Unfortunately, compound interest can work against you too. If you borrow money, the bank might charge you 10% or more. However, if you fall behind on your payments, the balance just grows because of interest charges. The interest charges are even higher the next month because they are charging interest on the interest. If you fail to make a minimum payment and get hit with a penalty, you will continue to pay interest on the penalty amount too.

It can be difficult to dig yourself out of this hole, so be careful with your spending.

More Tips on Credit Cards

To keep your life simple, I recommend you just use one or two credit cards for most of your expenses. Look for a card that offers at least 1% cash back and has no annual fee. If you use one credit card, you'll only have one bill to pay at the end of the month and you can track your spending easily.

If you can manage your spending and pay your credit card bills on time, you can consider having a company card with the retailers or businesses with whom you spend the most money. If you spend $500 per month on Amazon, consider using the Amazon card and earning cash back on your purchases. The promotions may change over time, but currently, Amazon offers 5% back on Amazon.com and Whole Foods purchases if you are also an Amazon Prime member. Other retailers offer similar rewards on everyday purchases if you use their credit card at their store. Target offers 5% back on purchases in their stores when you use their credit card. If you spend $500 per month on Amazon and Whole Foods, that is $6,000 per year. If you get 5% back on those purchases, that is $300 back in your pocket for the year. Compare this to what you get in a savings account: 1% interest on $6,000 in savings is only $60 for the year. Plus, you have to pay taxes on that measly $60. Interest from a savings account is generally taxed as ordinary income. If you pay a 22% tax, then you only keep $46.80.

When you get cash back from your credit card, that money is not taxed. So the $300 you got in a cash back reward is the equivalent of earning $426 at your job if you pay around 30% on your income. (In some rare instances, sign-up bonus rewards can be taxed, but they are generally not taxed if you are earning rewards on your spending.)

0% Interest Credit Cards

If you have a lot of credit card debt, contemplate getting a new credit card with a 0% rate for a year. You may be able to transfer your old balance to the new credit card and avoid some of the interest charges. Just make sure you are using this as an opportunity to pay down your debt, not as an excuse to spend more and add to your debt. I discuss a few circumstances where it may make sense to use credit cards to exploit some other investments, but the best advice is usually to reduce spending where you can and avoid credit card debt.

More Ways to Get Cash

The best way to find extra money for investing is to earn more money or cut back on expenses. But there are other ways.

You could sell your car and buy or lease a cheaper one, or even live without one for a while (if you live in a city where this is an option). These possibilities would give you some extra money to invest.

You can sell some other things that you don't need. Do you have any watches or jewelry or books or collectibles that are just collecting dust? Leather jackets or brand-name clothing? Expensive handbags? You might be able to make some serious money by selling on eBay, Amazon, or other online platforms. If you have luxury goods, you can check out therealreal.com, and research other sites as well.

You might talk to your bank or credit union about a low-interest loan. You could talk to friends and family about your plans and see if you can get a loan from them. Perhaps take a second job to work a few hours on the weekend or do some freelance work. The method is up to you, but make every effort to pay off debt and start investing as soon as possible.

Key Takeaways

Avoid credit card debt if at all possible. Pay it off as soon as you can and find a credit card with a good cash back reward program. Paying off credit card debt can effectively give you a 20% (or higher) return; this is better than most investments that are available to you.

Chapter 9

Eliminating State Income Tax

We've been talking a lot about taxes in this book. Most of the discussion has focused on federal income tax and payroll taxes that virtually everyone pays when they have a job. However, there is at least one more big tax that can burden you on every paycheck and limit your ability to rapidly create wealth for yourself: state income tax.

State income taxes vary widely. These nine states have no income tax at all:

- Alaska
- Florida
- Nevada
- New Hampshire (taxes investment earnings but not earned wages)
- South Dakota
- Tennessee
- Texas
- Washington
- Wyoming

Many Americans are moving to low-tax states. If you choose to do this, you will be in good company. The trend has accelerated as more companies allow their employees to work remotely. Avoiding state income tax can help you to build more wealth in a shorter period of time.

If you're thinking about making a move, be aware of the pros and cons. States with no income tax often make up for the loss of revenue by charging residents higher sales, property, or excise tax. The excise tax can include things like fuel, tobacco, and alcohol.

For example, while Tennessee has no income tax, it has the highest combined sales tax rate in the nation at 9.53%, according to the Tax Foundation. Taxes are also linked to spending on things like public services, infrastructure, and education. Lower taxes can mean less spending on these items. On the other hand, the quality of a child's K-12 education is not necessarily determined by per-pupil spending by the state. In my experience, it usually has more to do with how well the local school district is managed and how dedicated the parents are to the education of their children.

Also, consider the overall cost of living in a particular location and how much that may affect your wages. You may find more affordable real estate by leaving a big city, but the pay might be less too.

Determine how much a state may tax your investment income. California taxes income at a higher rate than most other states, *and* taxes capital gains as regular income. It does not make a distinction between short-term and long-term capital gains. This means your capital gains taxes could be between 1% and 13.3%, depending on your overall income level. Even if you make just $58,635 and file as single, you will be subject to a 9.3% capital gains tax there.

If you are a California resident and sell an investment property outside of the state and have a capital gain, you will still need to pay taxes to the state just because you are a current resident. It doesn't matter if you were a resident of the other state when you bought the investment property.

If you're just starting your career, state income tax may not be a big factor in your life. However, it will be a much bigger issue when your income rises and when you have more investment income. I want you to plan to be rich, so it is best to think about these issues now in the same way you consider other investment decisions discussed in this book.

If you can find an equivalent job and cost of living when you move to a state with no income tax, you are making a home run investment in yourself and your future. If you can save 5% or 10% of your income by avoiding a high state income tax, that is HUGE. It will allow you to build your wealth much faster than you could in a high-tax state.

Suppose that you earn $50,000 per year and no longer need to pay a 5% state income tax. Instead, you invest that extra money in a mutual fund that earns 8% per year. Let's assume that your income goes up by 2% every year and you continue to put 5% of your income into this investment. **If you start at age 25 and finish at age 65, you would have $883,762 in this account**. What if you avoid a 10% state income tax and invest the savings in this example? At age 65, you would have **$1,767,524 in this account**. Are you starting to see why people are moving to states with no income tax?

The Tax Haven of Puerto Rico

If you're already seriously thinking about relocating to reduce taxes, you might consider Puerto Rico. As a resident, you may be able to drastically reduce your taxes and build wealth more quickly than you ever thought possible. I am going to give you an overview of the benefits in this chapter, but be sure to consult with an expert if you want to consider a move to Puerto Rico.

Puerto Rico is a US Commonwealth—part of the US but independent in some ways. The Puerto Rico tax system is a hybrid. If you can move yourself and/or your business, you may be able to drastically cut your income taxes. The interaction between the IRS and the tax collectors in Puerto Rico is nuanced. It requires some Puerto Ricans to file with the IRS, some with the Puerto Rico Department of Finance, and some with both agencies.

Puerto Rico has successfully lured over many American mainlanders with its income tax of just 4%. Additionally, there is no tax on dividends and no capital gain tax in Puerto Rico. But, you must be careful. You cannot easily avoid US tax on the appreciation of your assets *before* you move. If you move with appreciated stock or other property and then sell, all the appreciation you had before the move is still subject to US tax; only your post-move appreciation will be subject to the special tax rates in Puerto Rico. You generally must wait a full 10 years to sell after you move to escape US tax on all pre-move appreciation. If you sell your US real estate, it is fully taxed in the US no matter how long you might be in Puerto Rico.

There are some specifics you should understand if you are willing to move to Puerto Rico and live there for ten years. There is a 5% tax on long-term capital gains realized before becoming a resident of Puerto Rico but recognized after 10 years of becoming a resident of Puerto Rico—as long as your Puerto Rico residency is recognized before January 1, 2036. This 5% long-term capital gain tax applies to just the portion of the gain in the asset while the individual lived outside Puerto Rico. If the long-term capital gain is not recognized within these periods, the applicable individual long-term capital gain rate would apply to any Puerto Rico-sourced long-term capital gain.

For some types of assets, you may not want to be locked in for ten years. But for people who have most of their wealth invested in index funds that they plan to hold until they die, it may not be much of a burden to hold them for ten more years.

To take advantage of the tax breaks, your real home must be in Puerto Rico. If possible, sell your old home, move your family, and sever any connections that could make it look like you still live there.

To qualify, you must not have been a resident of Puerto Rico within the last 15 years, and you must become a resident of Puerto Rico by December 31, 2035. You need to reside there for at least 183 days a year. You also need to handle the paperwork and file an application with the tax authority there. If you successfully make the move, you will receive big benefits:

- No tax on dividends that are earned after becoming a resident

- No long-term capital gains tax on appreciation after becoming a resident

- 5% tax on long-term capital gain for appreciation before you move for any sales during your first 10 years as a resident

What is the Catch?

Moving to Puerto Rico is a significant life change, and there are plenty of potential pitfalls. You will face some strict labor laws and regulations if your business has employees. You may experience some culture shock trying to fit into a place quite different from the mainland United States. Spanish is the first language for most of the people on the island, and it can be hit with major hurricanes. It may not be easy to find work depending on your background and preferred career.

However, for independent people that are self-employed and don't mind making some significant adjustments in their life, it could be a dream tax haven and a great way to accelerate your wealth-building. **Be sure to consult with an expert advisor in this field if you are considering a move to Puerto Rico to make sure you are aware of any rules and regulations that may not be included in this book.**

Personal Confession

Here is my confession: I still live in California. My wife and I both grew up here and we have family here. Our kids won't be out of the house for many years, and some things in life are more important than the state's income tax. However, the day will come when the kids are in college and we have less of a need to be in California. You'd better believe that when that day comes, we will begin researching relocation options to states with no income tax.

> ### Key Takeaways
>
> Be careful in deciding where you want to settle down and start a career. You might be better off financially if you live in a state with no income tax; the long-term benefit could be in the millions of dollars.

Chapter 10

Put It All Together & Make Millions

Now that you understand the concept of home run investments, let's look at two scenarios. In the first, our hero, Aaron, uses his benefits and wealth-building strategies to create increased wealth over time.

In the second scenario, we meet Bill. Bill fails to take advantage of these benefits and gets left in the dust compared to Aaron. Think of Bill as someone who works for a big company but doesn't understand the company's benefits and doesn't want the "hassle" of managing different investments or spending accounts. Or, you can imagine Bill as an employee without strong company benefits.

The average college grad earns about $50,000, so that's the income level we'll give to both Aaron and Bill. We will assume that their income increases 2% each year. Starting at age 25, Aaron does the following to build wealth:

- Contributes 5% to his 401(k) and gets a 4% employer match.

- Chooses to live in a state with no income tax. He is so happy about the money he is saving that he decides to invest an extra 5% into his 401(k). The equivalent of 14% of his salary is now going into his retirement account.

- Uses a conventional 401(k) with immediate tax savings. He invests in an index fund that earns 8% per year. He takes the immediate tax savings and invests it in a separate (taxable) account that earns 7% after taxes.

- Contributes 10% of his pay to his company's ESPP. He uses the 10% contribution for his daily expenses when he sells the stock each quarter, but he invests the 17.6% profit into an index fund earning 7% per year after taxes.

- Contributes $750 per year to a health care FSA. This amount goes up with inflation of 2% each year. He uses up the $750 on health care needs and invests the tax savings into an index fund earning 7% per year after taxes.

- Contributes $5,000 per year to a dependent care FSA from age 25 to 35 to pay for day care and nanny expenses for two kids over 10 years. He uses up the $5,000 each year and invests the tax savings into an index fund earning 7% per year after taxes.

- Aaron starts with no money in the bank. He works until age 65 and keeps up with this strategy every year.

- Assume he only saves and invests the money shown here and uses the rest of his income for general living expenses.

Let's look at this chart to see what happens over 40 years.

Age	Salary	Annual 401k Contribution	401k Balance	Separate Investment Account Balance	Combined net worth
25	$50,000	$5,000	$ 7,000	$ 3,685	$ 10,685
26	$51,000	$5,100	$ 14,700	$ 7,672	$ 22,372
27	$52,020	$5,202	$ 23,159	$ 11,983	$ 35,141
28	$53,060	$5,306	$ 32,440	$ 16,641	$ 49,081
29	$54,122	$5,412	$ 42,612	$ 21,672	$ 64,285
30	$55,204	$5,520	$ 53,750	$ 27,104	$ 80,853
31	$56,308	$5,631	$ 65,933	$ 32,964	$ 98,896
32	$57,434	$5,743	$ 79,248	$ 39,283	$ 118,532
33	$58,583	$5,858	$ 93,790	$ 46,096	$ 139,886
34	$59,755	$5,975	$ 109,659	$ 53,437	$ 163,096
35	$60,950	$6,095	$ 126,964	$ 59,863	$ 186,827
36	$62,169	$6,217	$ 145,825	$ 66,791	$ 212,616
37	$63,412	$6,341	$ 166,369	$ 74,260	$ 240,629
38	$64,680	$6,468	$ 188,733	$ 82,307	$ 271,041
39	$65,974	$6,597	$ 213,068	$ 90,975	$ 304,043
40	$67,293	$6,729	$ 239,535	$ 100,307	$ 339,842
41	$68,639	$6,864	$ 268,307	$ 110,352	$ 378,659
42	$70,012	$7,001	$ 299,574	$ 121,160	$ 420,734
43	$71,412	$7,141	$ 333,537	$ 132,787	$ 466,324
44	$72,841	$7,284	$ 370,418	$ 145,291	$ 515,708
45	$74,297	$7,430	$ 410,453	$ 158,734	$ 569,186
46	$75,783	$7,578	$ 453,899	$ 173,183	$ 627,082
47	$77,299	$7,730	$ 501,033	$ 188,711	$ 689,743
48	$78,845	$7,884	$ 552,153	$ 205,393	$ 757,547
49	$80,422	$8,042	$ 607,585	$ 223,313	$ 830,898
50	$82,030	$8,203	$ 667,676	$ 242,558	$ 910,234
51	$83,671	$8,367	$ 732,804	$ 263,223	$ 996,027
52	$85,344	$8,534	$ 803,376	$ 285,408	$ 1,088,784
53	$87,051	$8,705	$ 879,834	$ 309,221	$ 1,189,054
54	$88,792	$8,879	$ 962,651	$ 334,777	$ 1,297,428
55	$90,568	$9,057	$ 1,052,343	$ 362,201	$ 1,414,544
56	$92,379	$9,238	$ 1,149,463	$ 391,624	$ 1,541,087
57	$94,227	$9,423	$ 1,254,612	$ 423,188	$ 1,677,800
58	$96,112	$9,611	$ 1,368,437	$ 457,045	$ 1,825,481
59	$98,034	$9,803	$ 1,491,636	$ 493,356	$ 1,984,992
60	$99,994	$9,999	$ 1,624,967	$ 532,295	$ 2,157,262
61	$101,994	$10,199	$ 1,769,243	$ 574,049	$ 2,343,292
62	$104,034	$10,403	$ 1,925,347	$ 618,815	$ 2,544,162
63	$106,115	$10,611	$ 2,094,231	$ 666,806	$ 2,761,037
64	$108,237	$10,824	$ 2,276,923	$ 718,250	$ 2,995,173
65	$110,402	$11,040	$ 2,474,533	$ 773,390	$ **3,247,923**

Aaron will be a multimillionaire in retirement—not bad for someone who started with an annual income of $50,000 and only got a small raise each year! At age 52, he reaches a net worth of $1 million. It took 27 years to make his first million. It takes a long time to get there, but after he reaches $1 million, his wealth-building ability increases much more rapidly as the wealth continues to compound. Just eight years later, he reaches $2 million in savings. In five more years, he has over $3 million.

Keep in mind that this is just a "middle-of-the-road" example that shows the benefit of a few employee benefits. The outcome would be even better if we included additional wealth from a health savings account and the potential tax savings on commuter benefits. It will be easier to save and invest more if and when your income increases (beyond the $50,000 in this example). If we started this example with a salary of $70,000 and a 15% contribution to the 401(k), Aaron would have $5.9 million at age 65!

An Example of What Not to Do

Let's take a closer look at what Bill does and does not invest in.

- Contributes 5% to his 401(k) and gets a 4% employer match.
- Chooses to live in a state with a high state income tax. This limits his ability to save additional money in his 401(k) and his other savings.
- Uses a conventional 401(k) with immediate tax savings. He invests in an index fund that earns 8% per year. He takes the immediate tax savings and invests it in a separate (taxable) account that earns 7% after taxes.
- Works at a job that does not have an ESPP program (or maybe it does, but he just didn't want to "bother with it").
- His job does not have a health care FSA or a dependent care FSA (or maybe they offered it and he just didn't want to manage his cash spending through these accounts).
- Bill, too, starts with no money in the bank, works until age 65, and keeps up with this saving plan every year.
- Assume he only saves and invests the money shown here and uses the rest of his income for general living expenses.

Let's review the chart below to see how Bill does.

Age	Salary	401k Contribution	401k Balance	Separate Investment account Balance	Combined net worth
25	$50,000	$2,500	$ 4,500	$ 550	$ 5,050
26	$51,000	$2,550	$ 9,450	$ 1,150	$ 10,600
27	$52,020	$2,601	$ 14,888	$ 1,802	$ 16,690
28	$53,060	$2,653	$ 20,854	$ 2,512	$ 23,366
29	$54,122	$2,706	$ 27,394	$ 3,283	$ 30,677
30	$55,204	$2,760	$ 34,553	$ 4,120	$ 38,674
31	$56,308	$2,815	$ 42,385	$ 5,028	$ 47,413
32	$57,434	$2,872	$ 50,945	$ 6,012	$ 56,957
33	$58,583	$2,929	$ 60,293	$ 7,077	$ 67,370
34	$59,755	$2,988	$ 70,495	$ 8,230	$ 78,725
35	$60,950	$3,047	$ 81,620	$ 9,476	$ 91,096
36	$62,169	$3,108	$ 93,745	$ 10,823	$ 104,568
37	$63,412	$3,171	$ 106,951	$ 12,279	$ 119,230
38	$64,680	$3,234	$ 121,329	$ 13,850	$ 135,178
39	$65,974	$3,299	$ 136,973	$ 15,545	$ 152,517
40	$67,293	$3,365	$ 153,987	$ 17,373	$ 171,360
41	$68,639	$3,432	$ 172,483	$ 19,344	$ 191,828
42	$70,012	$3,501	$ 192,583	$ 21,469	$ 214,052
43	$71,412	$3,571	$ 214,417	$ 23,757	$ 238,174
44	$72,841	$3,642	$ 238,126	$ 26,221	$ 264,347
45	$74,297	$3,715	$ 263,863	$ 28,874	$ 292,736
46	$75,783	$3,789	$ 291,792	$ 31,729	$ 323,521
47	$77,299	$3,865	$ 322,092	$ 34,800	$ 356,892
48	$78,845	$3,942	$ 354,956	$ 38,103	$ 393,059
49	$80,422	$4,021	$ 390,590	$ 41,655	$ 432,245
50	$82,030	$4,102	$ 429,220	$ 45,473	$ 474,693
51	$83,671	$4,184	$ 471,088	$ 49,577	$ 520,665
52	$85,344	$4,267	$ 516,456	$ 53,986	$ 570,442
53	$87,051	$4,353	$ 565,607	$ 58,723	$ 624,330
54	$88,792	$4,440	$ 618,847	$ 63,810	$ 682,657
55	$90,568	$4,528	$ 676,506	$ 69,273	$ 745,779
56	$92,379	$4,619	$ 738,941	$ 75,138	$ 814,079
57	$94,227	$4,711	$ 806,536	$ 81,434	$ 887,971
58	$96,112	$4,806	$ 879,709	$ 88,192	$ 967,901
59	$98,034	$4,902	$ 958,909	$ 95,444	$ 1,054,353
60	$99,994	$5,000	$ 1,044,621	$ 103,225	$ 1,147,846
61	$101,994	$5,100	$ 1,137,371	$ 111,572	$ 1,248,943
62	$104,034	$5,202	$ 1,237,723	$ 120,527	$ 1,358,250
63	$106,115	$5,306	$ 1,346,291	$ 130,131	$ 1,476,422
64	$108,237	$5,412	$ 1,463,736	$ 140,431	$ 1,604,167
65	$110,402	$5,520	$ 1,590,771	$ 151,475	$ **1,742,246**

You can see that Bill falls far behind Aaron. By age 59, Bill is still able to accumulate $1 million in savings. When he retires at age 65, he has $1.7 million. He may be able to enjoy retirement, but his net worth is roughly half of what Aaron was able to achieve because Aaron exploited multiple home run investments. He was able to accumulate much more wealth without any more risk with his investments. He planned ahead and positioned himself in a job (and a state) that had a few extra perks that he could use.

I'm being a bit generous with Bill to give you an "apples-to-apples" comparison. In the real world, most of the "Bills" in the workforce are not consistently saving 5% every year for 40 years and getting an employer match. They are typically starting to save later in life and saving inconsistently. They may be working for employers that do not offer a 401(k) match, and they may be selling their stock investments at the wrong time, earning much less than 8% on their investments. Most of the "Bills" will end up with nowhere close to $1 million in retirement. However, this example does show you the power of compound interest and employer matching, even if you don't do anything else right in your investments.

Ask and You Shall Receive

There is an old story about a married couple that took a long cruise on a big cruise ship. They saved up for years to afford the trip. They believed the food would be expensive, so they packed up their food, survived on cheese and crackers for most of the trip, and just ate in their room. On the last night of the trip, they decided to let loose and have dinner in the main hall and just pay whatever it cost. They had an amazing meal, and at the end of the night, they asked their server for the check. The server replied, "All the food on the cruise ship is free! It's included with the cost of your ticket!"

We are all surrounded by amazing opportunities and even free benefits if we just take a moment to look for and ask about them. There are millions of hardworking employees all over the United States that could be building wealth every pay period, but they have not been seeking the right opportunities. Millions more are working in jobs without benefits who would be better off applying to jobs that offer the benefits and opportunities presented in this book. All they need to do is look.

Key Takeaways

Do everything in your power to start saving and investing early, reduce your taxes, and exploit the benefits that are offered to you. Anyone can do it.

PART 2

BUILD GENERATIONAL WEALTH

Chapter 11

Real Estate: Own Your Home

Buying a home is a big decision and it can be a great investment in building generational wealth. This chapter covers the best-case scenario for buying a house to make sure you understand what all the excitement is about and how it could be a profitable long-term investment. Keep in mind that the information relating to housing and taxes applies specifically to the United States.

People generally recommend buying a home for the following reasons:

- Mortgage interest tax deductions

- You can benefit from an increase in the value of your home

- You can use leverage to make a bigger profit

- Selling your house for a profit and sometimes paying no tax on the profit

We will discuss all of these in detail.

Mortgage Interest Deduction

When you buy a home, you generally take out a loan with a bank called a *mortgage*. The bank will usually require 20% of the purchase price of the home as a down payment. That means that for an $800,000 house, you need to have $160,000 in cash. If your loan is 3.5% on a 30-year fixed mortgage, your mortgage payment is $2,873 each month. In the first month, $1,866.67 is paid as interest on the loan and $1,006.33 is the amount of the principal that you are paying off each month. When you pay down the principal, you are building equity in the home. The eventual goal is to pay off all the debt, at which point your equity becomes the value of the house.

In the first year, you will pay a total of $22,204.40 in interest and $12,271.60 in principle. That is a lot of money coming out of your pocket. The good news is that you now get to deduct the interest payments from your taxes—meaning that you don't need to pay federal income tax on $22,204.40 of your earnings that year.

Understanding Taxes and the Standard Deduction

We should pause for a minute to dive deeper into taxes and a thing called the *standard deduction*. If you have a job and rent your home, you are probably taking the standard deduction. In 2022, the standard deduction is $12,950 for a single person, $25,900 for a married couple, and $19,400 for a head of household.

You can either take the standard deduction or *itemize* deductions on your taxes, but you cannot do both. Itemized deductions are expenses allowed by the IRS that decrease your taxable income. This approach can save you a significant amount of money over time.

Taking the standard deduction means you cannot deduct home mortgage interest or take certain other tax deductions. If you itemize, keep records and receipts supporting your deductions in case you are audited by the IRS. You should also be aware of the restrictions on some deductions; if you have medical expenses, you can only deduct the portion that exceeds 7.5% of your adjusted gross income. You should consult with an accountant if you have any questions on your deductions.

Back to our home-buying example. Because we had $22,204.40 in mortgage interest, it would now make sense as a single person to itemize your tax deductions. But the true tax benefit of owning the house and having a mortgage is only the difference between the standard deduction at $12,950 and the mortgage interest at $22,204.40. The additional tax deduction is $9,654.40. If you pay 22% in federal income tax, the net tax benefit is $2,035.97 for the year. I am showing this example for a single person to keep the numbers simple and show the potential benefit. But keep in mind that a married couple who is renting would get a standard deduction of $25,900, which is greater than the mortgage interest in this example.

Be aware that you can only deduct interest on $700,000 in mortgage debt. There is no additional tax deduction for the interest you pay beyond the first $700,000. (I chose an example here that puts us close to the $700,000 limit).

The good news is that once you itemize, you can deduct other items from your taxes. The next big deduction you may have is the state and local tax (SALT) deduction. You can deduct up to $10,000 in state and local tax payments from your federal income tax.

How Does the SALT Deduction Work?

This SALT deduction can include property, income, and sales taxes. Anyone who itemizes can deduct property taxes, but you must choose between deducting income tax or sales taxes. Most choose to deduct income taxes because those payments are usually greater than sales tax payments. If you are in a state with a high income tax, you are likely going to use the state and local income tax. However, if you are in a state with no income tax, you will probably opt to deduct your sales tax payments. Be aware that even if you pay much more than $10,000 in state and local taxes, the deduction is capped at $10,000. The $10,000 limit applies to single filers, joint filers, and heads of households. The deduction has a cap of $5,000 if your filing status is married filing separately.

Before buying a house, fully understand your income and tax situation. If you have a high income in a state with a high state income tax, you will benefit more from the mortgage interest deduction and itemizing your taxes. The tax benefit of the mortgage interest deduction was just $2,035.97 in our example above. But now you get the added benefit of the SALT deduction. If you are in the 22% tax bracket, you could save an additional $2,200 on your taxes assuming a $10,000 SALT deduction. The combined tax benefit is now $4,235.97. Not bad! You need to determine whether this financial benefit is enough of a reason to push you toward buying a house. You should also consult with an account-ant to make sure you understand your unique situation.

Side Note on Tax Laws: In 2017, some tax laws changed so that there were fewer incentives to buy a house and carry a big mortgage. The mortgage interest cap was reduced from $1,000,000 to $700,000. Taxpayers were given a larger standard deduction so that most people would pay less in taxes even if they didn't have a mortgage or a need to itemize their taxes.

Let's stick with this best-case scenario and show what hap-pens if you sell your house for a profit. In this example, you bought the house for $800,000. Let's assume that after 10 years, the house doubled in value and is now worth $1,600,000. (While this is not a typical performance, we can assume we got lucky.) When you sell an asset like a stock or mutual fund, you normally need to pay a capital gains tax on your profit. But your primary residence gets special treatment in the tax code. If you are single, you will pay no capital gains tax on the first $250,000 of profit. Married couples will pay no capital gains tax on the first $500,000 of profit. That is a *very* good deal. By comparison, if you sold some stock with an $800,000 profit, you would pay a capital gains tax on the entire profit.

Your down payment was $160,000 and the profit is now $800,000. That is an excellent return on your initial investment! The return is high because you were able to use leverage to in-vest. You borrowed 80% of the home value when you bought it, but you get to keep most of the profit when you sell.

Home Ownership Forces You to Save

You can find studies that show homeowners accumulate much more wealth over time than renters. There are a lot of reasons this may be true. In some cases, property values can go up quickly and suddenly you have much more wealth.

However, if you live in an area where property values have not increased significantly over the years, there is still another reason why you may be better off financially than your neighbors who rent: A typical mortgage builds equity every month in your property. It is a type of forced savings. In our example here, the home buyer started off paying down $12,271.60 in debt each year. That is money you are putting back into your pocket and that you will eventually be able to cash in when you sell the house or refinance your mortgage.

Most people are not great at saving. There is always a temptation to just spend what you earn and not worry about the future. If a mortgage forces more people to save more money than they normally would on their own, that is a good thing. Just don't fool yourself into thinking that buying a house will automatically make you rich. There may be better uses for your money over the next few years—that is what this book is all about.

My advice is that if you are already maximizing your 401(k) employer match and other programs like ESPPs and you are taking steps to reduce your taxes, you may be in a good position to buy a home if you don't stretch yourself too much financially.

But beware of the worst-case scenario . . .

Why You Might Not Buy a Home

Real estate can be an excellent investment. It can also be a money-losing venture for some homeowners compared to renting. Even though many people see owning their home as a ticket to greater financial security, be aware of potential pitfalls.

Below is a brief list of the potential positives and negatives of owning your own home.

Positives:

- Your home may significantly increase in value
- The bank lends you money, so you have leverage if the property value increases
- In many cases, you get a tax deduction based on owning and having a mortgage

- When you are done paying off your mortgage, you own the property with no debt and no other rental obligation

- Every month you are paying down the loan, forcing you to "save" by creating equity in your home

- You have greater peace of mind knowing that your landlord cannot raise the rent or force you to move, and your monthly costs are mostly fixed

- You can make upgrades and repairs to the home and change it how you wish

Negatives:

- Your home may decrease or stay flat in value. It could also increase in value very slowly and underperform your other savings and investments.

- The bank lends you money so you have leverage, but you can also lose more money if your house decreases in value.

- Your mortgage interest tax deduction has been limited in recent years and may not be worth as much as you think.

- The total cost of home ownership may be higher than renting since you are now paying down the debt, maintaining the house, and paying for all other expenses.

- You are essentially locked into this property for the long-term, it may make it more difficult to move if you have a new job opportunity or some other reason. You can sell if you need to move, but it can be costly to do that. You can also rent the property to someone else, but there's no guarantee that the rent will cover all your costs or that you will get tenants that take care of your home.

In some parts of the country, property values have increased steadily over time. In other parts, property values have been flat or negative. Research your local market. Websites like Zillow and Redfin may help you understand the local market. Keep in mind that there are no guarantees that past trends will continue.

A Brief History of Housing in the Twenty-First Century

Over the years leading up to the year 2000, the stock market experienced a huge rally. Many stocks were overvalued, resulting in a bubble that eventually burst in 2000 and 2001. People started to sell their stocks as they watched their investments fall in value. Many people shifted more money into real estate as an alternative to the stock market. They bought their first home, bought a bigger home, or bought an investment property. Interest rates were relatively low, and the rates kept falling—giving buyers easy access to money. In the early stages of 2001 and 2002, there were probably a fair number of bargains around the country where you could buy a property, rent it out, and earn a profit as a landlord. The cost of owning was less than what your renter was paying, so your costs were covered if you had a good renter. In some cases, you could have a positive cash flow with just a 20% down payment.

So many people were buying real estate with low interest rates during this time that the home prices got bid up higher and higher. In many cases, rents were flat or going down because interest rates were low and fewer people wanted to rent. An existing property owner could refinance their loan at a lower rate and suddenly offer lower rents to new tenants depending on local market conditions.

This housing bubble started to burst in 2007 and 2008. People were buying empty houses speculating that the value of the house would go up and they could sell it later to another buyer for a profit. But eventually, there were too few buyers (and not enough renters to fill some of these properties), and the owners of the properties began to default. Property values fell dramatically. Many people were wiped out financially or at least lost their initial investment or down payment. On top of that, we ended up with a recession where people lost their jobs and banks started to fail because they owned too much of this risky mortgage debt.

That is a *very* brief history of the housing market in the early twenty-first century. The Federal Reserve tried to solve the problem by cutting interest rates again to encourage new buyers to purchase foreclosed homes. Interest rates were held low because this also encourages business investment and stock market investment. While I'm oversimplifying a bit here, I'm showing you some of the reasons that interest rates are so low and why your savings account earns less than 1%.

When interest rates are low, it means that investors are hungry for any kind of consistent rate of return above 1% or 2%. After the housing crash of 2008 and 2009, investors continued buying up all kinds of properties because they couldn't get a very good rate of return on bonds, savings accounts, or other traditional investments. Instead, they might have chosen to invest in single-family homes.

If an investor buys a house for $500,000, they may only get $2,000 in rent for it each month. The investor needs to pay for property insurance, property tax, landscaping, repairs and maintenance, homeowner association dues, and a lot of other expenses. This might add up to $500 per month—making the net profit only $1,500 per month (assuming the buyer paid all cash and has no mortgage).

So even after making this $500,000 investment, the owner may only net about $18,000 in profit for the year. That is a 3.6% annual return on your investment—not a lot of money considering the time it takes to manage a property and the risk you take if home values fall or if there is some disaster or unexpected major expense. After all, an investor could typically expect to make 8% or more in the stock market.

Why Would This Investor Want to Own a House?

Despite these seemingly high risks and low returns, investment properties are still attractive for a few reasons. An investor may be speculating that the house value will increase over time. If this does happen and they sell the house, they may be able to reinvest the money into another property without paying a capital gains tax (called a 1031 exchange if you do it with an investment property). They may be speculating that rents will rise and they can get more profit from that. They may already own a lot of stocks and bonds and just want some diversification in their assets. Ultimately, the investor is desperate for a higher yield. Just like you, they can't even get a 1% return on their savings account.

This desperation for a higher yield on our investments is creating unusual conditions in the housing market. People are paying more for an asset than they normally would.

I want you to understand some of the reasons why home prices are so high. If you decide to buy that $500,000 house in the example, you might put down 20%, which is $100,000. Your mortgage is now $400,000. If you get a 3.5% loan, your monthly mortgage payment will be $1,796. If you need to pay the extra $500 in miscellaneous costs discussed above, your total monthly expense is around $2,300 per month. You might decide that there is something better you can do with that $100,000 (especially after reading this book!).

If you decide that you are getting a good deal on the rent you're currently paying and you don't want to buy a home, that is just fine. Conditions could change and you may be ready to buy in the future.

Homeowner-Alternative Scenario

We looked at the best-case scenario for home ownership. Now let's look at an example where the homeowner does not get the benefits they had hoped for.

Suppose we have a person that makes $50,000 per year and buys a house for $300,000. The down payment on the house is $60,000 and the mortgage is $240,000. If the interest rate is 3.5% on a 30-year fixed mortgage, the total mortgage interest deduction is $8,326.72 in the first year. So far, she is well below the standard deduction of $12,950.

Let's assume she lives in a state where taxes are relatively low, so her SALT deduction is only $4,000 for the year. The total for these deductions is now $12,326.72. That means her itemized deductions are below the standard deduction of $12,950. (She could benefit from other itemized deductions like the charitable deduction, but we will ignore that in this example for simplicity.)

Now, let's assume that she bought her house in a town where house prices are stagnant. The value of the house just stays where it is for the next ten years. If she sells, she won't owe any capital gains taxes, but she also will not have a gain to tax. She will have paid down about $25,000 of debt. This *is* a type of forced savings, but keep in mind that if she had found a good rental deal, she could still have saved an equivalent amount of money in an investment account. Plus, she probably spent somewhere between $10,000 and $20,000 on repairs, maintenance, and general upkeep over 10 years. If, for instance, an air conditioning unit breaks down, it could be $5,000 or more for a replacement. When she sells the house, she will probably need to pay out a least 5% of the purchase price in realtor fees and other costs; $15,000 in this case.

She will recover her $60,000 down payment, but sadly, this money did not give her much of a return on her investment for 10 years. If she had invested that $60,000 in the stock market and it had gone up 8% each year, she would have had $129,535 at the end of ten years. In this example, the homeowner lost out on that opportunity to invest the original $60,000 in a more profitable asset.

This scenario has a negative outlook, but it is not completely unrealistic. These two scenarios are intended to make you aware of the potential risks and rewards. And this wasn't even the worst-case scenario. The $300,000 house could have fallen in value to $200,000 over the time this person owned it. In that case, all the down payment money is wiped out and the owner would owe more money in debt than what the house is worth. This is what happened in the 2008 financial crisis—and could happen again if we face a major recession or a housing bubble in the future.

Final Thoughts

If you decide to buy a home, be sure you are making an informed decision and are aware of the risks and alternatives. Certainly, there is a connection between home ownership and wealth; in the long run, you are probably better off owning a home. But there are no guarantees, and you shouldn't buy a home just because your friends and family are telling you to do it or because you've always heard that it's a good financial decision. Research home values and rental values where you want to buy and decide what is right for you.

Key Takeaways

Home ownership can provide an excellent opportunity to build wealth and reduce your taxes. Just be aware that there are no guarantees you will make a profit from owning a home.

Chapter 12

Pensions

A pension plan is a retirement plan where an employee adds money into a fund that includes contributions by the employer. The worker's pension payments in retirement are determined by how long the employee worked at the company and the annual income they earned on the job leading up to retirement.

In a pension plan, the company sets aside a fixed percentage of the employee's salary in a retirement savings account and invests the account proceeds on the worker's behalf. Over time, the invested assets increase in value and should provide the employee with a reasonable source of income in retirement. Usually, at retirement age, the employee can choose to receive those pension benefits as a lump sum or in a series of steady, annuity-like payments during retirement.

Pension plans are calculated based on three main criteria:

- The employee's years of service at the company or organization

- The employee's age

- The employee's annual compensation

According to pensionrights.org, about 20% of employees in the US participate in a pension. For private-sector workers, it's only 12%. However, for public-sector workers, it is 76%. You are much more likely to find a job with a pension if you work for the government.

Most private companies have embraced the 401(k) model covered earlier since this allows individuals to build wealth and manage their contributions. There are pros and cons to the 401(k) system. One challenge is that you must manage your own money. In a pension, a team of professionals manages the fund to make sure that you get a promised benefit once you retire. Employers that provide a pension can still offer a 401(k) or 403(b). Even if you have a strong pension benefit, be sure to take advantage of these other accounts to assist in your wealth creation.

Taxes on Pensions

Most pension plans are taxable, and you'll want to fully understand the potential tax rate on your future benefits.

You may be able to work with your employer to figure out if it is best to have taxes taken out of your pension plan payments during retirement. If you contributed after-tax cash to a pension, a portion of those proceeds could be tax-free. Consult with your employer or a professional accountant to make sure you understand the specifics of your situation.

Pensions versus 401(k)s

If you are enrolled in a pension plan, you do not make any investment decisions. Your employer manages the pension plan for the employees, makes all investment decisions, and disburses pension plan assets to the employees upon retirement. Employers also decide how much you need to invest in the pension. You have fewer choices than with a 401(k) plan. Both defined contribution (401(k)) and defined benefit (pension) plans have similar features, like tax-deferred growth and employer-matching provisions.

Pension Vesting

Vesting is defined as the amount of pension plan proceeds to which an employee is entitled, based on their time working for the company or organization. Pension benefits can vest right away or can be spread out over many years. If you have a pension plan, research the details of when you are eligible to receive benefits.

Pension plan participants also need to weigh vesting options if they are considering changing jobs. An employee may not want to leave a job if he or she is fully vested, because that could negatively impact his or her pension benefit in retirement.

There are two common types of forms of pension plan vesting, "cliff" and "graded."

Cliff Vesting

With a cliff-vested pension plan, an employee would typically lose their pension plan proceeds if they left the company before the vesting period, which is usually five to seven years. If the employee leaves the job after reaching the vesting period, they will get the full pension based on the time worked for the employer.

Graded Vesting

In a graded-pension plan, the employee is entitled to at least 20% of their pension plan proceeds after three years on the job. Another 20% is added into the pension plan for every additional year with the company, up to the fully vested year amount, where the employee would receive 100% of the pension benefit.

Public/Government Pensions

If you are researching employers or career paths, it's useful to be aware of the major types of employers that offer a pension benefit. It is a consideration when evaluating who to work for and how long you might stay there. A few types of jobs and industries where there is typically a pension benefit are:

- School teachers
- Federal government employees
- Military service members
- City and state employees

There is some doubt about whether all government employees will be able to collect their full pension benefits. Many city and state administrations have promised more than they can afford, and have not been contributing enough money into the pension assets to take care of everyone in retirement.

A full discussion of pension benefits and risks is beyond the scope of this book. However, do your research before starting a new job. If there is potential for a large pension benefit when you retire, research the specific pension fund and make sure it's well funded with minimal risk of running out of money.

Private Companies with Pensions

Companies that offer pensions may be a dying breed. Most do not want the responsibility. Even some companies that provide pensions are transitioning newer workers into 401(k) plans.

But in some cases, the company will offer a fully funded pension benefit without any contribution (or payroll deduction) required from the employee. It is a great benefit if you can find a company that offers this.

Below is a list of a few employers that may still offer a strong pension benefit:

- 3M
- Aflac
- BB&T
- Coca-Cola
- ExxonMobil
- Johnson & Johnson
- NextEra Energy
- NuStar Energy
- Southern Company
- United Parcel Service

I won't classify a pension as a home run investment since your pension may not guarantee a specific rate of return. Some retirees may face challenges with their pensions down the road if the pension has not been managed well. A pension is a nice benefit to have, but don't rely on it as your sole source of future income.

Key Takeaways

Pensions are more common in government jobs. Understand this benefit if you are considering working for an employer that offers a pension. A pension can create a reliable stream of income when you are older.

Chapter 13

Custodial Accounts

If you have children, consider opening a custodial account for them so they can begin to learn more about investing. This can also help you save money on your taxes.

If your child does not have taxable income or wages, you can open a custodial brokerage account for him or her. The account will initially be in your name, but your child will be able to take control of it once he or she reaches age 18 or 21, depending on what state you live in.

You want a brokerage account with a good online platform and no account fees or minimum initial deposit. This will give your kids the chance to start investing with a small amount of money. I have had good experiences with Fidelity and Vanguard. You might start with those two companies if you want to keep it simple.

You may want to teach your children about investing in individual stocks, but I recommend you keep most of the money in low-cost index funds that can grow over time with minimal involvement from you.

When funds are transferred into a minor child's custodial account, the funds belong to that child. The parent can still function as the account's custodian/manager, but can only use the money for expenses that benefit that child. Parents are legally forbidden from using custodial account money for expenditures that benefit themselves. In some cases, it can be tough to distinguish between expenditures that benefit a child and those that benefit the parents or other family members. It may be rare for a child to dispute a withdrawal, but do your best to manage the funds according to the rules and laws that govern the account.

Tax Benefits

In 2022, a child can receive up to $1,150 in unearned income tax-free in a custodial account. The next $1,150 is taxable at the child's tax rate, which is usually much lower than the parent's tax rate. The tax that the child pays is sometimes referred to as the "kiddie tax." Figuring out the kiddie tax can get complicated in some circumstances, so you may want to consult with an accountant. Any earnings over $2,300 are taxed at the parent's rate.

Suppose your child can save 15% in taxes on their first $1,150 of investment income each year. That is an annual savings of $172.50 every year. That is a significant amount of savings for you and your child. By now, you've learned that any time you can make money tax-free, take advantage of it as a wealth-building tool. If your child is old enough to understand something about taxes, you can explain this benefit to them. I am sure your children will appreciate the extra $172.50 in their account and the fact that you set it up for them!

Anyone can give a monetary gift of up to $16,000 per year (or $32,000 per couple) to a recipient without incurring a federal gift tax. This rule applies to custodial accounts as well as other forms of gifts.

Be aware that a custodial account can have an impact on financial aid for college. Research your situation and determine how much money you want to contribute to a 529 college savings plan versus a custodial account.

After our son was born, my wife's parents gave us some money for him. There were no strings attached, but they asked us to save it for his future. It sat in a savings account for a long time. I finally told my wife that we should invest it in something simple like an S&P 500 index fund. We could add to it over time if we got more cash gifts, and it would be a way for our son to learn about investing when he got a little older. When I first told my wife about a custodial account, she was on board, but later, she seemed a bit concerned.

What if he ends up with $50,000 or $100,000 in the account by the time he's an adult and he wastes it all? she asked.

If he wastes it all, I said, *it will be a valuable lesson. If he does something foolish with $50,000, that might stop him from doing something foolish with his entire inheritance down the road. Lots of successful people have a story from their early days about a bad investment or a failed business. What if he does something great with the money? Maybe he will start a successful business or make a down payment on a house with the money.*

My wife was convinced, and we opened the custodial account a week later.

Gifts and Taxes

There are some restrictions on giving people cash gifts. Suppose you give a child or grandchild $20,000 this year. This gift exceeds the annual exempt amount by $4,000 and would require special care. The amount over the $16,000 annual limit would be deducted from your $12.06 million lifetime gift and estate tax exemption. Unless you have already used up this lifetime exemption, you won't owe any tax on the gifts to the child, but you will still need to let the IRS know that those gifts exceeded the annual limit by filing a gift tax return. In this case, your lifetime gift exemption is reduced by a total of $4,000. The good news is that neither the giver nor the recipient needs to pay any taxes on the money unless you exceed the $12.06 million lifetime gift exemption.

If you have made it this far into the book and end up using several of these wealth-building strategies, I recommend you find a good accountant that can answer any questions about your situation and help you minimize taxes and maximize your wealth.

Key Takeaways

Opening a custodial account is an excellent way to help your children save money and learn about investing. It is another opportunity to reduce your taxes and build wealth for future generations.

Chapter 14

529 College Savings Plans

If you have a child and want to save for college, consider opening a 529 college savings plan. Although contributions are not tax-deductible, earnings in a 529 plan grow tax-free and will not be taxed when funds are withdrawn to pay for qualified education expenses—tuition and fees, books, supplies, and some room and board costs. It can also pay for $10,000 in K-12 tuition per year and up to $10,000 in student loan repayment per beneficiary and per child.

Many states offer a state income tax deduction or credit for 529 plan contributions, so look up the rules in your home state. Usually, you can exclude qualified 529 plan distributions from your taxable income when you are ready to spend the money on college expenses.

You can open up a 529 account with almost any investment company. If you don't already have an investment account, start by looking at Vanguard and Fidelity. You can link the 529 to your regular checking account and make automatic payments each month if that suits your needs and makes it easier to keep up with contributions.

When our son turned one year old, a friend of mine asked me what I was getting him for his birthday. I said I was opening a college savings account for him. She looked at me a little strangely. Wasn't I supposed to spend a couple of hours at a toy store to buy an expensive toy to amuse my child and impress everyone at the party? I'm sure that is what a lot of people do. Our little one would be happy with a new book or shiny rock. But I think my son will thank me later when he has a lot of money to spend on college and little or no student debt to worry about. A one-year-old boy can't even say "thank you." Why should I buy an expensive toy? He won't even appreciate it until he turns two!

I have college savings accounts for my two children that I manage with Vanguard. Look into different types of investment funds and decide what is right for you. I generally recommend a low-maintenance type of fund that targets the child's high school graduation date. I use a "Vanguard Target Enrollment" fund for the year the child will enroll in college. A target-date fund like this will automatically invest in more conservative types of investments as you get closer to the graduation date, so you are less likely to see a sudden drop in the value of the fund if the stock market takes a dive near the graduation date.

High Contribution Limits

Unlike other savings plans, such as an IRA, 529 plans have no annual contribution limits and have high aggregate limits—ranging from $235,000 to $529,000, depending on the state. This means the total value of the contributions cannot exceed these levels. But it can grow higher based on the earnings and compound interest.

How Does Giving to a 529 Plan Affect the Gift Tax?

If you wish to help fund a 529 college savings plan, the $16,000 annual gift still applies; however, in this case, you can bundle five years' worth of $16,000 gift tax exemptions into an initial $80,000 contribution to one child's 529 plan. Keep in mind that any additional gifts to that individual during the next five years will put you over the annual giving limit, so your lifetime exclusion will be reduced by the additional amounts.

The Power of the 529 Plan

The tax benefit of the 529 plan can pay off in a big way over the period that you are saving for college. Let's assume you start saving $500 per month (or $6,000 per year) when the child is one year old, and you stop contributing when he or she turns 18. Also assume you are in the 32% tax bracket and that you earn 8% on your investment. That is 17 years of growth with no taxes on the profit.

After 17 years, you'll have $202,501, or $41,374 more in a tax-deferred 529 account than a taxable account. This is because a taxable return of 8% shrinks to 5.44% after taxes, based on your federal tax rate of 32%.

Year	529 Savings Account	Taxable account
Year 1	$6,000	$6,000
Year 2	$12,480	$12,326
Year 3	$19,478	$18,997
Year 4	$27,037	$26,030
Year 5	$35,200	$33,446
Year 6	$44,016	$41,266
Year 7	$53,537	$49,511
Year 8	$63,820	$58,204
Year 9	$74,925	$67,370
Year 10	$86,919	$77,035
Year 11	$99,873	$87,226
Year 12	$113,863	$97,971
Year 13	$128,972	$109,301
Year 14	$145,290	$121,247
Year 15	$162,913	$133,843
Year 16	$181,946	$147,124
Year 17	$202,501	$161,127

This calculation is based on the Vanguard college savings calculator. Plug in your own numbers at their website:

https://vanguard.wealthmsi.com/ collsavings.php

Financial Aid Considerations

When a dependent student or their parent owns a 529 plan, it is reported as a parental asset and therefore could have an impact on financial aid eligibility. Any distributions from parent and student-owned accounts are not counted as income on the Free Application for Federal Student Aid (FAFSA). A 529 plan offers the same benefit to all families, regardless of household income. You can choose any type of 529 plan, and it does not matter in which state the child eventually attends college.

Penalty for Non-Qualified Withdrawals

If you withdraw from the fund for a non-qualified distribution, the money is subject to income tax and a 10% penalty on the earnings portion of the distribution. There are exceptions to the penalty if the beneficiary gets a scholarship, attends a US military academy, dies, or becomes disabled. Only put money into the account that you plan to use for college and be aware of the penalties if you try to access the money too early. The 529 plans are similar to an IRA or 401(k) in this way.

Ownership Rules

The 529 plan account owner (usually a parent), not the beneficiary (the child/student), is the one in control of the money. The account owner can change the beneficiary at any time, which could mean shifting to another child that plans to go to college. The owner can also take a non-qualified distribution and even liquidate the plan if they need access to the money in the account. Just watch out for the taxes and penalties.

State Income Tax Recapture

If a 529 plan account owner does a rollover into another state's 529 plan, any state income tax deductions and credits previously claimed may be subject to taxation. The earnings portion of the outbound rollover may be added back to state taxable income, so consult with an expert if you are considering this. It is probably in your best interest to just keep it simple and avoid unnecessary taxes if possible.

Avoiding Fees

Watch out for any 529 plan fees that reduce the return on investment. Direct-sold 529 plans are generally less expensive than advisor-sold 529 plans. Research options and find a low-cost 529 plan option that meets your college savings needs.

Flexibility in Spending

Funds from a 529 plan can even be used for some apprenticeship programs, trade schools, or continuing education programs. Parents can also use leftover funds in a 529 account to further their own education or repay up to $10,000 in student loan debt.

Generational Wealth

The 529 plans are an example of using money to build generational wealth. If your child does not use all the money in the account, it can be left there indefinitely. You can let the money grow and compound over another 20 or 30 or 40 years until you have a grandchild ready to go to college. At that point, the grandchild can become the beneficiary and the funds can be used for his or her college expenses. Imagine the benefits of having this extra money growing over time, benefiting future generations—and doing so without paying taxes on the investment.

Maybe there is an uncle or aunt or grandparent in the family that would like to stop buying toys for the child and instead make contributions to a 529 plan. You can set it up so that they can make contributions every month or every year. What a great way to invest in education and help future generations!

Key Takeaway:

If you set aside some money for college savings in a 529 plan, you can get a nice tax break on the investment profits and build significantly more wealth over time. You also create a great benefit for your children and even your grandchildren.

Chapter 15

Student Debt

You may be wondering what you should do if you have a great deal of student loan debt. Should you still be contributing to all these tax-advantaged accounts, even when you have debt to pay off? Yes. Absolutely.

Unless you are completely drowning in debt, incurring fees and penalties, and can't pay your monthly living expenses, you should do everything you can to take advantage of the benefits in this book. The average student loan interest rate in the United States is about 6%. I have been explaining easy ways for you to earn anywhere from 15% to 100% on your money with a minimal amount of risk. You don't need to rush to pay down your student loans extra quickly if you have other ways to invest the money that give you a better return on your cash; even if you need to make student loan payments over a longer period, you can come out ahead if you are investing your money well.

Depending on your income, you can deduct up to $2,500 in student loan interest payments on your federal income tax. If you are in the 22% tax bracket, that could reduce your taxes by $550. If your student loan payments are manageable, you may be better off paying the debt down slowly and maximizing the tax savings. Again, make sure you are not incurring any late fees or penalties.

Some employers offer aid to repay student loan debt. See if any company you are interested in working for offers this benefit since it could have an impact on where you decide to work.

I won't devote a lot of space here to student loans, but from what I have observed, most people get into trouble here when they stop making payments for a while and then get hit with late fees and penalties. This increases their future interest payments and makes it even harder to get out of debt. As we discussed in the credit card chapter, compound interest can work *against* you too.

Do everything you can to avoid paying late fees and penalties on your student loans, credit cards, and all other forms of debt. If you think your interest rate is too high, consider consolidating or refinancing your student loan debt to make your payments more manageable. This could make it easier for you to build wealth with my strategies.

The other way that people get into trouble is when they don't have a clear plan to get a good-paying job with their new, expensive degree. Try to avoid this if it isn't too late.

Even if you are out of college and making money, consider living like a starving student for a few years if that will help you achieve your financial goals. I had roommates all through college and for two years after college because I knew I could save money this way (even though I was getting tired of having roommates). A year after graduating from college, I quit my job and decided to take a pay cut to change industries. It was a difficult adjustment for the first few months, but I continued to save every dollar that I could to plan for a better future. I look back on that time and still think of it as one of the most fun periods of my life. I was surrounded by good friends that enjoyed hanging out together. None of us made much money. You don't need a lot of money to have a good time, and you will be happier if you are not adding to your debts with needless spending.

Key Takeaways

Avoid excessive student loans if you can. Try to keep from getting hit with late fees and penalties that will make it much more difficult to pay down your debt. Ensure you have a reasonable interest rate on your student loans. If you are not drowning in debt, do everything you can to save and invest in the programs I've outlined.

Chapter 16

Index Funds

If you have set up the investment accounts discussed in this book you may be wondering what you should invest your money in. In recent years, a huge number of intelligent investors and financial advisers have embraced *index funds*. Index funds are mutual funds that mirror the performance of the overall stock market and generally perform better than most other types of mutual funds.

A *mutual fund* is an investment vehicle made up of a pool of money collected from many investors to invest in stocks, bonds, and other assets. Mutual funds are operated by professional money managers who allocate the fund's assets and try to produce capital gains or income for the fund's investors.

Some of the most popular index funds invest in the entire stock market or the S&P 500. The S&P 500 is a stock market index that measures the performance of 500 companies in the United States. It includes companies across 11 sectors to offer a diversified picture of the health of the US stock market and the broader economy. Consider the Vanguard 500 Index Admiral Fund (VFIAX) as one of your investments. It mirrors the performance of the S&P 500, and the expense ratio is only 0.04%. This allows you to own shares in 500 of the biggest and best companies in the United States. Index funds typically keep the fees as low as possible to improve the performance of your investment. This is significant—many actively managed funds will charge you a much higher rate for investing your money.

Many investors think of the stock market as a type of casino. They want to pick winning stocks and mutual funds because they think they can get rich quickly or outsmart the market. The reality is that almost no one can consistently beat the market over several years. Even if you think you have found an advisor or fund manager that has beaten the market, it is nearly impossible to know whether they have just been lucky or will be able to beat the market in the future.

If you invest in an actively managed mutual fund that is trying to beat the market, you could pay 1% to 2% of your assets in fees annually. This reduces your investment returns each year to pay for this active management. Because you are paying extra for this investment, the odds are even lower that you will be able to pick the right funds and beat the market after paying these extra fees. You may also end up paying higher taxes on the investment if the fund is frequently moving in and out of different stocks to take some quick profits.

Why is this so important? Consider what three different mutual funds are worth over 40 years. Let's go back to our classic example of an employee who earns $50,000 per year with 2% raises each year. He contributes 10% of his salary every year for 40 years (we will ignore any potential employer match or other benefits). What happens if he invests in a high-fee fund that underperforms with a net return of 6% after fees? What if he invests in a fund that earns 7% after fees? What if he invests in the index fund with super-low fees that returns 8% each year?

The 6% fund will leave him with $1,081,333.

The 7% fund will leave him with $1,377,047.

The 8% fund will leave him with $1,767,524.

An extra 1% or 2% will make a HUGE difference. The 8% fund leaves you with a balance 63% higher than the 6% fund! The 8% fund results in a balance that is 28% higher than the 7% fund. I hope by now you see why I am so obsessed with these percentages—and I hope you are getting obsessed, too.

Too many people are invested in the types of funds that return 6% or 7% because they are trying to win a game that is virtually impossible to win. Do you really think you can beat the market for 40 years—*and* beat it by enough to make up for the increased cost in fees and taxes? You almost certainly cannot do this. The people who do this for a living are spending anywhere from 40 to 100 hours per week researching stocks and following the stock market. Many of them have advanced degrees in math and economics and decades of experience working in the industry. Even most of *them* are not able to consistently beat the market year after year. Good luck competing against them.

If you need more convincing on index funds, I recommend you read *Common Sense on Mutual Funds* by John Bogle and *Money: Master the Game* by Tony Robbins.

I won't label index funds as a home run investment since I can't guarantee specific performance on the dollars you invest. However, if you can earn (or save) an extra 1 to 2% on your money over many years, you will be well-positioned to build wealth.

Mental Strength

One of the keys to successful investing is maintaining the mental strength to stay invested despite the stock market's ups and downs. You don't necessarily need to be fully invested in the stock market; maybe you want 50% of your assets in stocks and 50% in bonds. The most important thing is to stick with your strategy and do not sell just because the market has dropped. Stay the course, and you will do well.

Another mutual fund worth considering is VBIAX, or the Vanguard Balanced Index Admiral fund. It invests roughly 60% in stocks and 40% in bonds. The fund rebalances automatically if stocks or bonds increase or decrease in value. Balanced funds like this may help you to sleep at night and ride out the ups and downs without selling at the wrong time. You can also consult with a professional financial advisor to create a balanced portfolio appropriate for your investment goals. If you work with a professional, make sure you understand the fees you are paying and try to keep those fees to a minimum.

Tony Robbins has written two books that focus a great deal on the concept of overcoming the human emotions that sabotage us when we invest. A second, shorter book I recommend is *Unshakeable*. In essence, Robbins recommends that nearly everyone invest in index funds and have patience with the stock market, even in a bad year. He points out that, on average, there is at least one significant correction (defined as a 10% drop) or a bear market (defined as a 20% or more drop) each year. As he points out, "winter is coming." It comes virtually every year. Just as winter eventually turns to spring, the stock market has always managed to recover from economic downturns. Try not to check your investments every day or even every week. Consider checking them once per month or once every few months and don't worry too much about what is driving stocks up or down on a given day.

People who hold onto their investments and put more money into stocks when they are undervalued have performed very well. If you invested $100 in the S&P 500 at the beginning of 1980, you would have $11,675 at the beginning of 2021, assuming you reinvested all dividends. This is a return on investment of 11,575% or 12.10% per year. Despite all the recessions and wars and economic crises we have endured over the last 40 years, the American economy has always managed to recover and reach new heights.

Consider advice from Warren Buffett, one of the richest men in the world and one of the most successful investors of all time. Buffett has instructed the trustee in charge of his estate to invest 90% of his money into the S&P 500, and 10% in treasury bills for his wife after he dies. Even very successful investors with a great track record of picking stocks see the wisdom in investing in index funds.

Key Takeaways

Try to use index funds for most of your investments. Avoid selling when the market is down. Stick with your strategy to save and invest every month.

CONCLUSION

I hope you have learned some new strategies to save money and increase your wealth creation in the months and years to come. I recommend you read at least one book on personal finance every few years. It will keep you focused on the right strategies and up-to-date on current tax laws. Also, your financial goals may change over the years. The advice you need at age 25 may be different from the advice you need at 45 or 55. **Investing in your knowledge is always a home run investment.**

I invite you to follow me online at:

www.trsmithinvests.com.

You can also receive email updates and follow me on social media. My username is @trsmithinvests on Instagram and TikTok.

Some of the material in this book is meant to build on what employers and human resource departments are conveying (or not conveying) in their benefits packages. In my experience, employers don't get employees excited enough to participate in programs that should be no-brainers. Many employees do not fully understand how much a quick profit on an investment means to their financial future. As you have read, this could come in the form of matching funds, discounted stock, a pretax deduction, or some other benefit. A dollar saved is a dollar earned, and the dollars in your investment account don't care whether they were earned or saved. Capture every extra dollar available to you.

Some people have mixed emotions about reducing their taxes because they want to fund important public services. All I can tell you is that these tax laws were written by the tax collectors (a.k.a., the government). The government provides incentives to encourage certain activities and investments, so take advantage of them. When more people save and invest and create wealth, it ultimately makes for a stronger society and creates more income and wealth for everyone. Are you going to spend more, give more to charity, and pay more in taxes if you are rich? Yes.

I would be thrilled if this book becomes a best seller among human resource managers and I hope they find ways to sell their company benefits to employees so that participation rates are much closer to 100%.

Many personal finance books teach you about amazing possibilities if you quit your corporate job and start your own business. All of that may be true. I have read many of these books, and they are very aspirational. But most people that read personal finance books are ultimately going to stick with a regular job with a salary and benefits. Make the most of your job **AND** the benefits!

Some Career Advice

I have worked in a few different industries, and I have seen a lot of my friends change jobs and change industries they work in. If you are miserable in a job, it is probably best to find a new one. However, I would recommend that you think hard before moving into a completely different career or industry just because your current boss is difficult, or the company is a bit dysfunctional and does not recognize your contributions. If you have an opportunity to take a job at a different company that will pay you more, it could be a great move for you. Perhaps that new job will offer some of the great benefits discussed in this book.

However, I have seen too many of my friends tread water and earn much lower pay because they switch to new careers and need to learn the ropes all over again. It is not always bad to start over. It can be exciting to be a beginner again, learn new things, and focus on new possibilities. But after a year or two in a new job, there is still a chance of becoming restless and having the urge to quit and go somewhere else. I have had that urge many times but realized there is a difference between having a bad day and having a bad job. If you decide to quit your job, make sure you are doing it for the right reasons.

Start Now

I once heard someone on TV say "your first million is the hardest." When I first heard that, I had to chuckle. It seemed like it would take me a hundred years to make my first million—never mind my second or third million. But then I did some calculations, and I realized it *was* possible. I just had to start right away, save as much as I could, and make a few smart decisions. Becoming a millionaire isn't hard. It is just math. It's just a matter of time if you make some good choices.

Earlier, we looked at an example where we put it all together and saw how much you can accumulate if you make the most of your savings and benefits. In that example, it still took 28 years to the first million. After that, it took just eight years to get to $2 million. It took just four more years to get to approximately $3 million. It is all part of the miracle of compound interest. Albert Einstein once said "Compound interest is the eighth wonder of the world. He who understands it, earns it. He who doesn't, pays it."

The work you do early on will pay big dividends in the future. You have a ton of potential that we barely even touched on. You could make some good real estate investments and get to your first million much sooner than expected. You can get a big raise or promotion and accelerate your savings. You could get married and combine your resources to reach some of your goals much sooner. There is no limit to your potential.

I cannot predict what the future looks like, but my guess is it will be filled with amazing new inventions we can't even imagine today. It will probably include things like widely available 3D printers, self-driving cars, improvements in education that bring down the costs for everyone, medical breakthroughs to prolong our lives, and much more. By owning stocks and mutual funds, you will own a piece of this future and all the profits that come with it.

So, get started now!

Contact Me

I would love to hear from you! If you enjoyed the book, please post a review on Amazon or another website. You can send me an email at: TRSmithinvests@gmail.com. I would love to know what you learned and what type of content you would like to see in the future.

ABOUT THE AUTHOR

T.R. Smith has been an investor since 1995. He has an MBA from the University of California, Berkeley, and has spent more than a decade working for public companies as a specialist in finance and real estate. He lives in Orange County, California, with his wife and two children. You can find him online at trsmithinvests.com or on Instagram and TikTok with the username @trsmithinvests.

www.ingramcontent.com/pod-product-compliance
Lightning Source LLC
Chambersburg PA
CBHW032006190326
41520CB00007B/376